What the
Science
of Reading
Says

Literacy
Strategies
for Grades 3-5

Laura Keisler, Ed.D.

D1597130

Shell
Education

Contributing Author

Erica Bowers, Ed.D.

Consultant

Jennifer Jump, M.A.

Publishing Credits

Corinne Burton, M.A.Ed., *President* and *Publisher*
Aubrie Nielsen, M.S.Ed., *EVP of Content Development*
Véronique Bos, *Vice President of Creative*
Kyra Ostendorf, M.Ed., *Publisher, professional books*
Cathy Hernandez, *Senior Content Manager*
Fabiola Sepulveda, *Junior Art Director*
Michelle Lee Lagerroos, *Interior Graphic Designer*
David Slayton, *Assistant Editor*

Image Credits

All images from iStock and/or Shutterstock.

Shell Education

A division of Teacher Created Materials
5482 Argosy Avenue
Huntington Beach, CA 92649
www.tcmpub.com/shell-education
ISBN 978-1-0876-9674-4
© 2024 Shell Educational Publishing, Inc.

Table of Contents

INTRODUCTION

What the Science of Reading Says

This book is one in a series of professional resources that provide teaching strategies aligned with the Science of Reading. The term the *Science of Reading* pervades the national conversation around the best literacy instruction for all students. The purpose of this series is to close the gap between the knowledge and understanding of what students need to become literate humans and the instructional practices in our schools. This gap is widely acknowledged yet remains intact. While research is available, journals are not easy to navigate. However, with concise resources that build understanding of the body of research and offer strategies aligned with that research, teachers can be equipped with the logical steps to find success. This book will help you navigate the important Science of Reading research and implement strategies based on that research in your classroom.

> The Science of Reading is the collection of excellent research that leads to the understanding of how students learn to read.

What is meant by the phrase *Science of Reading*? The Science of Reading is the collection of excellent research that leads to the understanding of how students learn to read. Research dedicated to understanding how we learn to read and write has been conducted for more than fifty years. This research has explored topics ranging from the skills needed to read and write, to the parts of the brain involved in reading development, to the best way to teach children how to read. The research clearly demonstrates the following: 1) the most effective early reading instruction includes an explicit, structured, phonics-based approach to word reading; and 2) reading comprehension relies on word reading (being able to decode individual words) and language comprehension (being able to understand what words and sentences mean).

According to the Report of the National Reading Panel (2000), a comprehensive literacy program should contain explicit skills instruction in phonemic awareness, phonics, fluency, vocabulary, and reading and language comprehension. Effective literacy instruction includes explicit instruction in all five of the components of reading plus writing. Ideally, this will occur in classrooms that emphasize and facilitate motivation for and engagement in reading through the use of a variety of authentic texts, authentic tasks, cooperative learning, and whole- and small-group instruction that connects reading to students' lived realities. Motivation and engagement are important considerations in our teaching. Cultural and linguistic relevance and responsiveness are essential. Authentic opportunities for speaking, listening, and writing are critical. Gradual release of responsibility is necessary to build independence and is an integral part of promoting a culture of literacy that students will embrace and take with them once they leave our care. Let us explore more closely what we can learn from the Science of Reading.

The Science of Reading: Models of Reading

The widely accepted model of the Simple View of Reading (SVR) proposed by Gough and Tunmer (1986) and later refined by Hoover and Gough (1990) depicts reading comprehension as the product of word recognition and language comprehension. This model of reading offers educators a simple, comprehensible way of organizing their understanding of the constructs that can predict successful literacy outcomes (Snow 2018). Hoover and Tunmer (2018) describe these constructs as:

- Word recognition: the ability to recognize printed words accurately and quickly to efficiently gain access to the appropriate word meanings contained in the internal mental lexicon.

- Language comprehension: the ability to extract and construct literal and inferred meaning from speech.

- Reading comprehension: the ability to extract and construct literal and inferred meaning from linguistic discourse represented in print.

Word Recognition
The ability to transform print into spoken language

$\times$

Language Comprehension
The ability to understand spoken language

$=$

Reading Comprehension

The Simple View of Reading

Later work (Hoover and Tunmer 2020; Scarborough 2001) further describes the crucial elements within each of these constructs by incorporating the best of what science tells us about how we read. Scarborough's Reading Rope identifies the underlying skills required for effective and efficient word recognition and language comprehension.

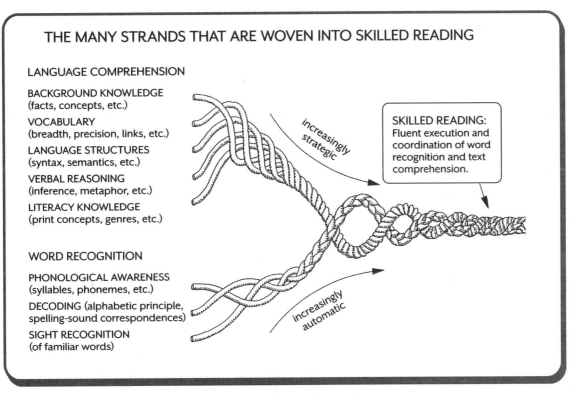

Scarborough's Reading Rope

Credit: Hollis Scarborough, "Connecting Early Language and Literacy to Later Reading (Dis)abilities: Evidence, Theory, and Practice" in *Handbook of Research in Early Literacy*, edited by Susan B. Neuman and David K. Dickinson © Guilford Press, 2001.

Wesley Hoover, William Tunmer, Philip Gough, and Hollis Scarborough are psychologists who dedicated their research to understanding what reading is and what must be present or learned for reading to occur. They have described the SVR as *simple* because it is intended to focus our attention only on what is important in reading, not to explain the process of *how* reading happens. Similarly, Scarborough expanded on the SVR to focus attention on more specific details of language comprehension and word recognition such as prior knowledge and phonological awareness, attempting to include space for process with the addition of automaticity and strategy. Both the SVR and the Reading Rope are models—hypotheses that attempt to explain the phenomena of reading. The models describe necessary but not sufficient conditions for reading. Many teachers know that decoding skills can be present, language comprehension can be apparent, and yet comprehension can be impeded. These foundational models do not account for motivation, development, social emotional considerations, linguistic differences, and a host of other factors relevant to literacy teaching and learning.

In the use and understanding of these models, one can see how the Science of Reading brings together expertise across disciplines. These models of skilled reading provide a roadmap for researchers and classroom educators for the development of instructional practices that promote these essential skills.

The Science of Reading: Implications for Teaching

Here is where we are wise to remember that the Science of Reading relies on the *sciences* of reading. It encompasses many fields. The modeling work of cognitive and educational psychologists informs the work of others in literacy research. The work of the literacy researchers informs the work of those who translate it into instructional practices. The end goal is to explain the processes by which successful reading occurs and the most effective ways to develop skills that enable these processes. As Louisa Moats declared, "Teaching reading is rocket science!" In this seminal piece, Moats describes how teachers can think about the Simple View of Reading in relation to their classroom practice:

> The implications of the Simple View of Reading should be self-evident: reading and language arts instruction must include deliberate, systematic, and explicit teaching of word recognition and must develop students' subject-matter knowledge, vocabulary, sentence comprehension, and familiarity with the language in written texts. Each of these larger skill domains depends on the integrity of its subskills. (Moats 2020, para. 11)

Moats's description reflects the recommendations of the National Reading Panel (NRP) (2000) and the modeling by cognitive scientists. The evidence base from the sciences that inform our understanding of reading consistently supports systematic and direct instruction in the five components of reading: phonemic awareness, phonics, fluency, vocabulary, and comprehension.

Phonological Awareness and Phonemic Awareness

Phonological awareness is an umbrella term that refers to noticing and manipulating sounds in speech, for instance, individual words, syllables, and sounds in words. *Phonemic awareness*, a subcategory of phonological awareness, is the understanding that spoken words are made of individual sounds called *phonemes*. Research demonstrates that phonemic awareness can be taught and that this teaching is effective for a variety of learners (NRP 2000; National Early Literacy Panel 2008). It assists children in learning to read and learning to spell. Explicitly teaching children to manipulate phonemes with letters, focused on one or two types of phoneme manipulations rather than multiple types, and teaching children in small groups are most effective (NRP 2000). According to the recommendations of the NRP report, preschool and kindergarten children should receive approximately 18 hours of phonemic awareness instruction to learn these skills. This means teaching phonemic awareness every day; 18 hours over the course of a school year is about 6 minutes per day. Phonemic awareness instruction should occur in grades 1 and 2 as needed.

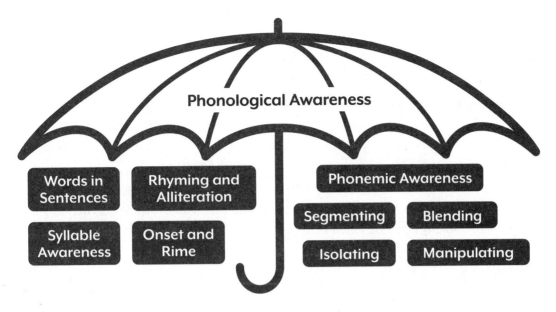

Phonics

Phonics is the term used to describe the relationships between the letters (graphemes) of written language and the individual sounds (phonemes) of spoken language. Phonics instruction helps children learn and use the alphabetic principle—the understanding that there are systematic and predictable relationships between written letters and spoken sounds (Armbruster, Lehr, and Osborn 2010). Children need knowledge of phonics to become efficient, automatic decoders of written text. Explicit, systematic instruction in phonics has been shown to be most effective (NRP 2000). Three complementary approaches should be used when teaching phonics: (1) *synthetic phonics*, which emphasizes teaching students to convert letters into sounds and then to blend sounds to form words; (2) *analytic phonics*, during which children do not pronounce sounds in isolation but rather learn to analyze letter-sound relationships in previously learned words; (3) *analogy-based phonics*, in which children learn to use parts of word families they know to recognize unknown words which may contain the same parts. Explicit and systematic instruction in phonics provides students instruction in letter-sound (grapheme-phoneme) connections. This graphophonemic knowledge is essential for mastery of decoding. Students must be provided instruction that engages the opportunity to hear, say, read, and spell words both in and out of context. This instruction should happen daily, for at least 30 to 45 minutes for students in grades K through 2. While not all children need intensive phonics instruction, no student is harmed by or will have their reading progress impeded by receiving phonics instruction. Most students will benefit significantly from systematic phonics instruction in grades K through 2.

> Children need knowledge of phonics to become efficient, automatic decoders of written text. Explicit, systematic instruction in phonics has been shown to be most effective.

Fluency

Fluency is defined as the ability to read with speed, accuracy, and proper expression. It is a critical component of skilled reading. Fluency depends upon well-developed word recognition skills readers can apply to silent reading or reading aloud that make word reading rapid, accurate, and cognitively efficient. When children are fluent readers, they spend less time trying to decode or pronounce words and can better attend to the comprehension of text. However, fluency also represents a level of expertise beyond word recognition (NRP 2000). Phrasing, intonation, and monitoring reading are all considered fluency skills. Research demonstrates that students benefit from fluency instruction and that reading comprehension may be aided by fluency (NRP 2000).

Vocabulary

Vocabulary refers to the words we must understand to communicate effectively. Vocabulary plays an important role in reading comprehension. Children who develop strong vocabularies and continue to deepen and broaden their vocabulary knowledge find it easier to comprehend more of what they read, especially as text becomes more complex (Sinatra, Zygouris-Coe, and Dasinger 2012). Moreover, students who have strong vocabularies have less difficulty learning unfamiliar words because those words are likely to be related to words that students already know (Rupley, Logan, and Nichols 1999). Researchers and educators often refer to and consider four types of vocabulary: *listening vocabulary* consists of the words we need to know to understand what we hear; *speaking vocabulary* consists of words we use to speak; *reading vocabulary* refers to the words we need to understand what we read; and *writing vocabulary* is the words we use in writing (Armbruster, Lehr, and Osborn 2010).

> Children who develop strong vocabularies and continue to deepen and broaden their vocabulary knowledge find it easier to comprehend more of what they read.

Research reveals that most vocabulary is learned indirectly, but some must be taught directly (Armbruster, Lehr, and Osborn 2010). Vocabulary instruction should be direct and explicit.

Comprehension

Research repeatedly demonstrates that students benefit greatly from both direct, explicit instruction in reading comprehension strategies and instruction in other areas that support reading comprehension (Duke, Ward, and Pearson 2021; Duke and Pearson 2002; Durkin 1978; Pressley and Afflerbach 1995). The NRP (2000) identified a number of effective strategies for teaching comprehension. These strategies include vocabulary development, prediction skills (including inferencing), the building of a broad base of topical knowledge, the activation of prior knowledge, think-alouds, visual representations, summarization, and questioning. Students also need to develop their metacognitive skills to become strategic and independent readers. Metacognitive skills, also referred to as *metacognition*, are most simply understood as thinking about one's thinking. This includes skills such as self-questioning, making connections, predicting, and visualizing. Most literacy researchers agree that metacognition plays a significant role in reading comprehension (Baker and Brown 1984; Gourgey 1998; Hacker, Dunlosky, and Graesser 1998; Palincsar and Brown 1987). Research shows that teachers should foster metacognition and comprehension monitoring during comprehension instruction, because in doing so, students will learn to monitor and self-regulate their ability to read.

Throughout this book, we delve more deeply into each of these areas to share and explain the research as it applies to specific areas of reading development and to students of different grade levels.

Components of Literacy

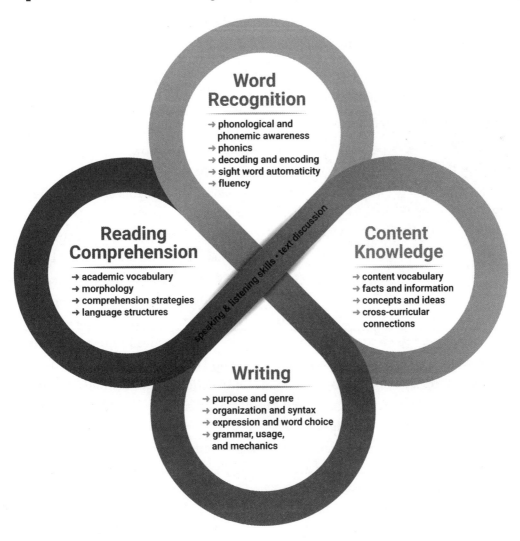

Word Recognition
→ phonological and phonemic awareness
→ phonics
→ decoding and encoding
→ sight word automaticity
→ fluency

Reading Comprehension
→ academic vocabulary
→ morphology
→ comprehension strategies
→ language structures

speaking & listening skills · text discussion

Content Knowledge
→ content vocabulary
→ facts and information
→ concepts and ideas
→ cross-curricular connections

Writing
→ purpose and genre
→ organization and syntax
→ expression and word choice
→ grammar, usage, and mechanics

The figure on page 7 reflects what we know to be the essential components of comprehensive literacy instruction. This visual representation of the Science of Reading brings together what we know from multiple sciences of reading and literacy, from research in early literacy, from research on the reading-writing connection, from the national reports on reading and literacy, and from the cognitive sciences. Development of skills in word recognition, comprehension, content knowledge, and writing are well supported in the research as effective practices for literacy instruction. The figure includes the five components of reading recommended by the National Reading Panel, however the reorganization of these components into the four constructs is intentional, representing the evolution in our understanding of the connections between reading and the wider consideration of what it means to be literate. Just as the SVR was intended to call our attention to the components of reading comprehension (Hoover and Tunmer 2022), the subcategories describing each component of this model give us guidance as to where to focus our teaching in order to support skilled reading and literacy development.

The inclusion of *content knowledge* as a separate construct is important in this model. Research has long struggled over the role of content knowledge in reading comprehension. We are well aware of the fact that the activation and development of prior knowledge (schema) is important to comprehension; we know that knowledge of words and word parts plays a key role in the decoding of new and/or unfamiliar words and determining the meaning of such words. Of primary importance for activating prior knowledge is the presence of relevant knowledge. There is a growing body of research that demonstrates the critical role of content knowledge in comprehension of text concerning that topic. In fact, the knowledge a reader brings (content and word knowledge) is the primary determinant of comprehension (Anderson and Pearson 1984; Cabell and Hwang 2020). Content knowledge can support readers in making inferences and connections to text. This can deepen understanding of a text and support learning as readers are better able to connect what they read in text to existing schema in ways that develop new learning (Cabell and Hwang 2020). Cabell and Hwang's recent review of research on content-rich literacy instruction (2020) demonstrates its important role in developing language and knowledge in support of reading comprehension. The inclusion of content knowledge as a separate and co-important construct in this model also serves as an important reminder that the Science of Reading goes beyond the narrow discussion of skills-based decoding instruction and that our literacy instruction should be embedded in meaningful context.

> There is a growing body of research that demonstrates the critical role of content knowledge in comprehension of text concerning that topic.

Including *writing* as a component in the model draws attention to the important role writing plays in literacy development and the reciprocal relationship writing shares with reading. Decades of research demonstrates that direct and explicit teaching of writing skills, strategies, and processes is effective at improving students' writing and communication skills (Graham et al. 2012b). There is great benefit to bringing reading and writing study and practice together (Graham 2020). Reading and writing draw from a shared set of literacy knowledge and skills, including vocabulary development, background knowledge, and an understanding of syntax, semantics, and morphology. Additionally, reading across genres to understand how one communicates in a particular genre can inform writing in that genre. Writing in response to reading makes comprehension "visible" as students summarize, explain, infer, and make connections to what they have read.

Finally, wrapping the components of this literacy model in a "ribbon" of speaking and listening serves as a powerful reminder that speaking and listening are essential to literacy development. Though reading and writing are not natural processes, our brains are hardwired for communicating through speaking and listening (Hulit, Howard, and Fahey 2018). Researchers and experienced educators can attest to the fact that listening comprehension skills and oral language abilities are generally more developed than students' reading and writing skills, particularly in younger children (Sticht and James 1984). Drawing on the stronger listening comprehension skills of young readers can enhance vocabulary development, grow knowledge of complex language structures, and aid content knowledge as students can comprehend through listening what they would not be able to read. Larger vocabularies and broad content knowledge in turn support reading comprehension and writing skills. As students' reading and writing skills progress, it is important that speaking and listening skills do the same. Speaking is directly connected to our thinking and learning. Opportunities to talk to others about our thoughts require us to be active in our thinking, making decisions about how to explain understanding and reflect on and analyze what we know or may not know. These conversations and discussions can help students make sense of new information and construct new meaning (Barnes and Todd 1995; Halliday 1975). Speaking and listening support the development of all other literacy skills, including reading comprehension and writing, and must be an essential element of effective literacy instruction.

> Speaking and listening support the development of all other literacy skills, including reading comprehension and writing, and must be an essential element of effective literacy instruction.

The model promotes literacy instruction that brings together multiple sciences of reading, with the ultimate goal of developing reading, writing, and communication.

Factors That Contribute to Reading and Writing Success

As mentioned above, success in reading and writing can be influenced by more than just explicit instruction in the components of literacy. Duke and Cartwright's (2021) Active View of Reading points to important factors that impact students, including cultural knowledge, motivation and engagement, and executive functioning skills. Each of these can be a determiner of student success. As well as addressing the needs of those students who are progressing at different rates, differentiation is essential for providing all students with the necessary tools for success. Many students enter our classrooms speaking a language other than English and need extra support while attaining English language proficiency. Below is a discussion of how teachers can create a supportive classroom environment and address these additional factors.

Motivating Students to Read

Ensuring that students are interested and engaged in the work of reading is one aspect of instruction that cannot be overlooked. Teachers must identify a range of ways to both engage and motivate their students.

> Ensuring that students have access to a wide range of texts will help each student find something to be passionate about.

INTERESTS

To foster a lifelong love for reading and writing that extends beyond the day-to-day literacy tasks of classroom life, teachers should become familiar with students' interests as early in the school year as possible with the goal of providing students with reading materials and writing assignments that are tailored to their interests, passions, and wonderings. Ensuring that students have access to a wide range of texts will help each student find something to be passionate about. Providing suggestions rather than rules about the types of texts to read allows for students to choose books that are informational, or contain poetry, or fables, or stories. Once these high-interest texts and assignments are made available, students are more likely to be self-motivated to read and write because they want to discover and share more about the topics that interest them. This self-motivated act of reading and writing develops students' desire to learn that is so important in accessing content from a wide range of texts and text types beyond their interests. Reading and writing about texts of interest allows students to fine-tune their skills in the context of experiences that are interesting, familiar, and comfortable for them, in turn providing them with the confidence and practice needed to effectively navigate texts that are more advanced, unfamiliar, or unexciting.

AUTHENTIC OPPORTUNITIES

There are several ways to offer authentic opportunities for students to purposefully engage with interesting texts. Challenge students to use reading to solve a problem, research something of interest, or compare characters they fall in love with. Reading challenges such as these can be formulated and scripted by the teacher, or they can be generic and allow for students to both create the pathway and discover the journey. For example, if a group of fifth-grade students shows interest in the civil rights movement after a social studies lesson, provide a text set for them to engage with. Have students choose which texts to read, which pathway to follow, and how they will share what they have learned. Similarly, if a group of third graders shows interest in a character, put together a bin of texts with similar characters. Provide students with the challenge: discover who is most interesting and prove it. These types of opportunities increase student time spent reading and writing. Without motivation, students will spend less time reading and writing, providing less opportunity to perfect literacy skills, build knowledge, and develop wide vocabulary.

OUTSIDE READING

In addition to discovering students' interests and providing suggestions and texts based on your findings, one of the easiest and most effective ways to improve reading comprehension and writing ability is to promote extensive reading outside of class. Students who frequently read a wide variety of materials have better vocabularies and better reading comprehension skills. They also can use those texts as models for future writing. As Randall Ryder and Michael Graves (2003) point out, wide reading fosters automaticity in students because it exposes them to more words in different contexts, provides them with knowledge on a variety of topics, and promotes lifelong reading habits.

A teacher's attitude toward reading and writing, especially for pleasure outside of school, has a tremendous effect on students in the classroom. Teachers who talk enthusiastically about books they have read and who model reading and writing as enjoyable and fulfilling experiences foster a love for reading and writing in their students. Teachers who can recommend books that are particularly engaging and interesting can increase student motivation tremendously. Teachers should have an intimate knowledge of reading materials for a wide range of abilities so they can recommend books to any student to read outside of class.

> Teachers who talk enthusiastically about books they have read and who model reading and writing as enjoyable, fulfilling experiences foster a love for reading and writing in their students.

THE CLASSROOM LIBRARY

A powerful step is to set up a classroom library. Why is it important to have a classroom library? According to Lesley Mandel Morrow (2003), children in classrooms with book collections read 50 percent more books than children in classrooms without such collections.

Teachers can collaborate with the school librarian or media specialist and parent organizations to build a sizeable collection of texts, which should be a mixture of fiction and nonfiction. Bear in mind that this library may serve to generate the interest to read about many different subjects, so providing students with a wide range of texts from which to choose will be beneficial in fostering their desire and motivation to read and write. Be sure to provide texts that are at your students' readiness levels along with texts that may present more of a challenge. Students can build their prior knowledge about a given topic at a less challenging reading level, preparing them to apply a variety of reading strategies to navigate more advanced texts on the same topic. Michael Pressley and his colleagues (2003) found that high-motivation and high-performing classrooms were, above all, filled with books at different levels of text difficulty.

The reading materials should be housed in bookcases that provide easy access for students to browse and choose books. Use tubs to hold magazines and articles on related topics and themes. Students will be better able to incorporate their new learning through independent reading into their existing prior knowledge if the materials are purposefully organized: science, science fiction, history, historical fiction, mystery, fantasy, adventure, and other types of literature.

> While we can entice students with carefully crafted libraries, success may still be hindered if we neglect to address their individual needs.

Once the materials are in place, create opportunities to incorporate them into your instruction. Assign projects and writing assignments that require students to use the classroom library materials to independently learn more about different topics. Also encourage wide reading by making independent and accountable reading a regular classroom activity. If students are not doing any reading outside of school, school should provide some time for students to read in class. It may be nearly impossible to imagine blocking out any time for silent reading in today's demanding classrooms, but as Stephen Krashen (2009) makes clear in his "81 Generalizations about Free Voluntary Reading," more reading leads to better reading, faster reading, better writing, more writing, and better language acquisition for English learners.

Motivation is one factor that impacts the successful development of reading and writing ability. While we can entice students with carefully crafted libraries, success may still be hindered if we neglect to address their individual needs. This means meeting students where they are and providing appropriate instruction and support, whether they are English learners, striving readers, or accelerated learners.

Differentiation

As teachers, we know that students come into our classrooms at varying reading, writing, and readiness levels to access the content at hand. Each strategy in this book offers suggestions for differentiating for various groups of students so that they can benefit from the strategy, whether those groups are English learners, striving (below grade level), or accelerated (above grade level) students. All students in our classrooms deserve access to rich and rigorous content. Differentiating the content, the process, the product, and the environment allows for all students to find success in learning to read and write.

> Differentiating the content, the process, the product, and the environment allows for all students to find success in learning to read and write.

Our goal is to help students acquire proficiency in reading and writing. As part of this goal, it is our responsibility to provide students with meaningful and interesting contexts to learn language and build their reading and writing skills. In doing so, teachers simultaneously aid in the development of students' collaborative, communicative, and group-based skills emphasized in speaking and listening standards, subsequently helping all students to strategically communicate and interact with those around them within the context of the English language.

English Learners

When implementing the strategies in this book, discuss with students the importance of using a variety of strategies to understand and write about new information that they glean from text. This helps students understand the importance of developing finely tuned reading and writing skills. The explicit instruction of these reading and writing strategies provides all learners with meaningful contexts for learning language, so this discussion is necessary for establishing a reason for reading and writing, not only for your English language learners, but for all of your students. Providing English learners with scaffolds for accessing content, developing literacy skills, and engaging with the context of unfamiliar cultural references builds pathways for students to find success. Giving English learners access to texts that will help develop their overall reading abilities is also essential to developing their writing skills. Ample opportunities to engage with rich content supports multilingual students in developing the knowledge and vocabulary that underpin their understanding. In addition, English learners "will benefit from actively seeking exposure to language and social interaction with others who can provide meaningful input in the second language.

Furthermore, they—and you, the teacher—can enhance students' English language skills by placing language learning in meaningful and interesting contexts" (Dunlap and Weisman 2006, 11).

Striving Learners

In addition to building motivation through interest-based texts, striving students will benefit from scaffolding. While all students benefit from explicit, authentic instruction, these are crucial elements for striving readers. Striving readers can benefit from participating in a small group before the whole-class lesson, which gives them the opportunity to learn the information in a lower-risk environment with text at a developmentally appropriate level. They may also need further practice with the content after instruction. It is vital that striving learners are provided with additional scaffolds to ensure their success.

Accelerated Learners

While it is critical to differentiate lessons for striving learners, accelerated students also benefit from modifications to instruction. Teachers can challenge accelerated learners by extending the content either in depth or breadth (Tomlinson 2014). In addition, teachers can provide accelerated learners with opportunities to demonstrate their understanding of content by modifying the process (how students are provided the content) or the product (what students produce to demonstrate understanding). Adapting curriculum for accelerated learners also addresses issues of motivation, as providing tasks that are cognitively challenging maintains their interest.

Throughout this text, we recommend differentiating the lessons to better accommodate all students. Some modalities we recommend are whole class, small groups, collaborative learning, and partner pairs.

Whole class may be used for:

- introducing a new strategy
- modeling think-alouds to show students how to use the strategy
- practicing think-alouds and allowing students to share their experiences and ideas using the strategy

Small groups may be used for:

- pre-teaching new strategies and vocabulary to English learners or striving students
- providing more intensive instruction for striving students

- checking students' understanding of how to apply strategies to the text they are reading or composing
- introducing accelerated students to a strategy so that they can apply it independently to more challenging texts
- encouraging students to use a strategy to think more deeply than they might have imagined possible

Collaborative learning may be used for:

- allowing students to practice strategies without teacher involvement (the teacher is available and "walking the room" to monitor group progress and understanding)
- providing striving students with peer support in completing tasks (when groups are strategically formed)

Pair students with partners to:

- strategically scaffold and support their learning (e.g., pair a striving student with a "near-peer"—someone who is just ahead of their partner)
- share responses and ideas when trying out strategies

Cultural Relevance

Students learn best when they feel they can take risks and be open to new experiences. For this to happen, teachers need to create a space where everyone feels valued and that they belong. One way to do this is to design a classroom that represents the diverse backgrounds and cultures of our students. Being mindful of students' home lives, cultures, and language experiences is known as being culturally and linguistically responsive. According to Sharroky Hollie, cultural and linguistic responsiveness (CLR) can be defined as the "validation and affirmation of the home (indigenous) culture and home language for the purposes of building and bridging the student to success in the culture of academia and mainstream society" (2018, 23).

Being a culturally and linguistically responsive educator is a journey. The concepts may be well-known, or they may be new. Culturally and linguistically responsive educators are self-aware and socially aware. They are aware of their own cultural backgrounds, which include ethnicity, nationality, religion, age, and gender, among other things. In the classroom, culturally and linguistically responsive educators are sensitive to cultural differences and have an unconditional positive regard for students and their cultures. They strive to continually learn

> In the classroom, culturally and linguistically responsive educators are sensitive to cultural differences and have an unconditional positive regard for students and their cultures.

about students and their cultures, adjusting their perspectives and practices to best serve students.

Culturally and linguistically responsive classrooms are print-rich and display the linguistic supports multilingual learners and others need to be successful. This includes the academic vocabulary that students are learning, which they need to access to be able to discuss language and content. In addition, these classrooms are active. Students utilize the four language components and are engaged in discussions with peers and teachers. They are physically active and move around the room to work with peers on a variety of projects. The materials being utilized reflect a variety of cultures and perspectives, and student work is prominently displayed and honored.

> Culturally and linguistically responsive educators design curriculum by selecting texts with characters and pictures that represent their students.

Culturally and linguistically responsive educators design curriculum by selecting texts with characters and pictures that represent their students. They create shared writing pieces that draw from the students' home languages and cultures. They encourage students to research areas of interest and produce art that validates and exhibits their cultures. Culturally and linguistically responsive educators are constantly reevaluating their curricular choices to ensure all students are represented and validated.

Hollie (2018) embraces a philosophy of affirming students' home cultures and languages and suggests educators "love outrageously." To be culturally and linguistically responsive, educators must know their students. When educators validate students' cultures and languages through classroom management and materials, they help students see themselves reflected in the curriculum and allow students to use their backgrounds to supplement the classroom learning environment.

Taking a culturally and linguistically responsive stance is a holistic approach. It embraces the whole learner. When students feel they belong, are validated, and are represented in the curriculum, they are open and connected to the learning. Teaching in this manner allows for everyone's story to be told.

How to Use This Book

This book includes a variety of strategies that can be integrated into any language arts curriculum to improve students' reading and writing skills: promoting word consciousness, analyzing word parts, activating and developing knowledge through vocabulary development and content learning, using think-alouds and monitoring comprehension, questioning, summarizing, using visual representations and mental imagery, using text structure and text features, incorporating mentor text, using graphic organizers, and modeling writing. These research-based instructional strategies will help teachers bridge the gap between the science of literacy instruction and classroom practice.

The strategies are presented in three sections: I) Word Recognition; II) Reading Comprehension and Content Knowledge; and III) Writing. These three sections correspond with three professional resources: *What the Science of Reading Says about Word Recognition* (Jump and Johnson 2023), *What the Science of Reading Says about Comprehension and Content Knowledge* (Jump and Kopp 2023), and *What the Science of Reading Says about Writing* (Jump and Wolfe 2023).

Each section opens with an overview of research in that area to emphasize the importance of that particular component. There is a clear and detailed explanation of the component, suggestions for instruction, and best practices. This information provides teachers with the solid foundation of knowledge to provide deeper, more meaningful instruction to their students.

Following each overview are a variety of instructional strategies to improve students' reading and writing. The strategies in the book include the following:

- background information that includes a description and purpose of the strategy, and the research basis for the strategy
- the objective of the strategy
- a detailed description of how to implement the strategy, including any special preparation that might be needed
- suggestions for differentiating instruction

When applicable, the strategy includes one or more activity sheets as reproducibles in this book and in the digital resources. Grade-level examples of how the strategy is applied are also included when applicable. For more information about the digital resources, see page 180.

SECTION I

Word Recognition

The strategies in this section correspond with key competencies identified in *What the Science of Reading Says about Word Recognition* (Jump and Johnson 2023). These research-based instructional strategies will help teachers bridge the gap between the science of literacy instruction and classroom practice.

Strategy	Skills and Understandings Addressed			
	Phonics	Beyond Foundational Phonics	Sight Word Automaticity	Fluency
Word Engineer Notebook	●	●	●	
Build Words with Prefixes	●	●	●	
Build Words with Suffixes	●	●	●	
Word Morph	●	●		
Beat the Clock			●	●
Word Sort	●	●		●
Word Break		●		
Phrased Reading				●

Word Recognition

In grades 3 through 5, readers' word knowledge develops, their store of words grows ever larger, and the quality of their knowledge of individual words improves over time. This furthers the automaticity in decoding that allows readers to devote cognitive processing resources toward comprehension of what they are reading (Perfetti 1995, 1998; Perfetti et al. 2007; Perfetti and Stafura 2013). Research suggests this applies to spelling and writing as well. When writers efficiently encode individual words, they keep track of the topic, organize their thoughts more effectively, and broaden their word choices, leading to better writing (Singer and Bashir 2004).

It is common for students in grades 3 through 5 to display a wide range of proficiency in the foundational skills of reading. Assessment and monitoring of these skills are critical components of effective instruction in these grade levels. Students with gaps in foundational skills need more instruction and support in these skills so they can access grade-level texts. When students struggle to access grade-level text, content learning is affected, as are reading motivation and reading for pleasure. Students who display proficiency do not need additional instruction. Differentiated instruction in foundational skills is essential so that students exit elementary school with strong reading skills. However, an integrated approach to word study, attending to the phonological, syntactic, semantic, and orthographic features of words, with opportunities to apply this knowledge in context, is recommended for all students through fifth grade (Bear et al. 2020; Toste, Williams, and Capin 2016).

> An integrated approach to word study, attending to the phonological, syntactic, semantic, and orthographic features of words, with opportunities to apply this knowledge in context, is recommended for all students through fifth grade.

Phonological and Phonemic Awareness

By and large, students in grades 3 through 5 do not need and will not benefit from instruction in print concepts and/or phonological and phonemic awareness. As students develop their reading skills, the importance of phonological and phonemic awareness decreases, though some research suggests students at beginning English proficiency levels and students with specific learning disabilities or specific phonological deficits may benefit from this instruction throughout the elementary years (Gutierrez and Vanderwood 2013; Moats 2022; Schmidt et al. 2021).

Phonics

Phonics instruction is teaching the relationships between sounds (phonemes) and letters (graphemes). The research is clear that children benefit from systematic and explicit instruction in phonics, regardless of the approach used to teach them (Ehri et al. 2001; National Early Literacy Panel 2008; NRP 2000; Snow and Juel 2005; Wanzek et al. 2018). Readers in grades 3 through 5 should receive instruction in grade-appropriate phonics skills addressing syllables and morphemes (including prefixes, suffixes, root, and base words). This knowledge will aid reading fluency and in turn, reading comprehension. Building on students' knowledge of phonics, instruction on patterns and exceptions can be useful. For example, knowing that *eigh* makes the long *a* sound in words like *weight*, *freight*, and *neighbor* while also knowing this pattern is an exception to the "*i* before *e* except after *c*" generalization.

As students advance through the upper elementary grades and beyond, the number of multisyllabic words in texts they read increases dramatically. Many of these words are not yet part of students' oral and/or listening vocabulary. Kearns and colleagues (2014) estimated that the number of multisyllabic words students encounter increases by more than 19,000 words year over year in grades 3, 4, and 5, reaching over 170,000 words by grade 5, a number the researchers admit may be an undercount.

Moreover, many multisyllabic words contain multiple morphemes, and knowledge of morphemes can aid in word recognition (Kearns et al. 2014; Nagy, Berninger, and Abbott 2006). Word study instruction that allows for multiple exposures to words and opportunities to manipulate words in isolation and in context, as opposed to strictly rules-based instruction, may be more effective (Toste, Williams, and Capin 2016).

Many of these multisyllabic words are rich in meaning and significant to the understanding of the text. As intermediate and advanced readers encounter increasingly complex text, continued instruction in phonics supports the decoding of unfamiliar multisyllabic words and eventually the storing of these words in memory, working toward automaticity in decoding and encoding.

> As intermediate and advanced readers encounter increasingly complex text, continued instruction in phonics supports the decoding of unfamiliar multisyllabic words and eventually the storing of these words in memory, working toward automaticity in decoding and encoding.

> Knowledge of words and word parts is essential to reading and spelling, and readers must be able to apply this knowledge accurately and efficiently.

Decoding and Encoding

Decoding words is a recognition task that involves the translation of print to speech, while encoding is a production task requiring the translation of speech to print (Murphy and Justice 2019). Considering the reciprocal nature of these processes is integral to word study. Knowledge of words and word parts is essential to reading and spelling, and readers must be able to apply this knowledge accurately and efficiently. An integrated word study approach as described throughout this section provides opportunities for the development of orthographic knowledge alongside the application of such word study to reading. The same grapheme-phoneme relationships readers rely on for word recognition in reading are called upon for spelling. Readers' ability to accurately map letters and letter combinations to sounds and store these in memory (a process referred to as *orthographic mapping*) is crucial to spelling development.

What do we do when we encounter unknown words? How do we apply our knowledge? Research tells us that more advanced readers strategically apply knowledge of morphemes and morphological parts to decode unfamiliar multisyllabic words, while poor readers tend to rely on pictures and context clues (Bhattacharya and Ehri 2004; Shefelbine and Calhoun 1991). In tandem with teaching knowledge of more complex words and word parts, older elementary readers benefit from systematic and explicit instruction in strategies for decoding these words—strategies that support readers in applying their word knowledge.

What about when the encounter with an unknown word is an encoding task, requiring one to spell a word, either mentally (e.g., when looking something up) or physically (when writing)? It is unlikely that memorizing the spelling of thousands of words is efficient, or even possible, so we need to be strategic. A focus on more complex word patterns and morphology has benefits for encoding, too. Effective spelling instruction is explicit about and takes advantage of the relationships between how words look, how they sound, and what they mean, integrating and enhancing readers' existing decoding knowledge and building strategies for word analysis.

Sight Word Automaticity

Proficient, competent adult readers have 30,000 to 60,000 sight words stored in their memories. A sight word is any word a reader can read automatically, without sounding it out. Sight words can be regular or irregular, high- or low-frequency words. As word proficiency continues to develop, sight words become words readers can spell and understand the meanings of with automaticity. Ehri (2014) and Kilpatrick (2015) suggest that the ability to read, pronounce, spell, and know word meanings by memory takes place through orthographic mapping. Explicit and systematic instruction in phonemic awareness and phonics in the early grades is essential for the facilitation of orthographic mapping. By third grade, with many of the foundational phonics skills in place, the process of orthographic mapping is central to developing advanced word recognition skills (Ehri 2014). Continued, repeated exposure to words through explicit instruction and word play is a must in the upper elementary years to build automaticity. Teachers of grades 3 to 5 would be wise to plan word study instruction in ways that foster automaticity and continue to build word reading skills in and out of context.

> Continued, repeated exposure to words through explicit instruction and word play is a must in the upper elementary years to build automaticity.

Fluency

As readers become increasingly strategic and increasingly automatic in their decoding, reading becomes more fluent (Scarborough 2001). Fluency is a measure of how accurately and quickly one reads. When fluent readers read aloud, their reading is accurate, at a quick but natural pace, and has expression. When fluent readers read silently, reading is highly automatic, with words grouped together for meaning rather than read word by word. Instruction that builds decoding skills and automaticity (described above) supports fluency. Additional explicit instruction and practice in pace, proper expression, vocabulary, and language structures (discussed later in this book) aid the development of fluent readers. In grades 3 through 5, students put the word recognition skills they learned in the primary grades into action as they become more fluent. It is critical we continue to attend to fluency as a foundational skill. When students leave elementary school with poor fluency skills, these issues tend to persist through middle and high school (Paige et al. 2014). Attention to accuracy and automaticity is important; however, we should not focus exclusively on reading rate (accurate word count per minute) as an indicator of fluency. In fact, one characteristic

of disfluent readers is reading text excessively fast, ignoring punctuation. When students attend to punctuation and read with expression (prosody), this can indicate comprehension; therefore, fluency instruction and practice should consider all three elements of fluency: accuracy, pace, and prosody. Wide reading, increasing reading volume, modeling of fluent reading, and repeated and assisted reading are all practices shown to support fluency (Rasinski et al. 2017).

Putting It All Together

By the time students reach grade 3, most have learned foundational skills and have a base in word recognition that allows them to read more independently, but as reading volume increases, the need to consolidate these skills is of critical importance. The development of strong orthographic representations and increasingly complex lexical knowledge paves the way for quick, accurate decoding and encoding, freeing up resources for comprehension and expression. Word study instruction that integrates decoding and encoding instruction and fluency instruction and practice is essential for continued development of advanced word recognition skills.

Word Engineer Notebook

Objectives

- Know and apply grade-level phonics and word analysis skills when decoding words.
- Use combined knowledge of all letter-sound correspondences, syllabication patterns, and morphology to accurately read unfamiliar multisyllabic words in context and out of context.

Background Information

Word study is critical as students become more advanced readers and is an essential companion to explicit skill instruction in phonics (Bear et al. 2020). Word study provides an opportunity for students to manipulate and play with words. One of the best ways for students to develop fast, accurate decoding and encoding skills is to engage students in meaningful reading and writing tasks and to provide multiple opportunities to engage with the same words out of context (Bear et al. 2020). Word Engineer notebooks provide this out-of-context practice. The more quickly students can decode and encode, the more their cognitive resources can be devoted to making meaning and producing meaning. The Word Engineer notebook is used year-round to develop and document both sight and meaning vocabulary, supporting students in becoming flexible, strategic readers. It centers on recognizing words by their orthographic and morphological features. Word Engineer notebooks may be used for several strategies in Sections I and II of this resource.

Materials

- spiral notebook or composition book, one for each student

Process

1. Provide each student with a composition book or spiral notebook.
2. Ask students to brainstorm what they know about engineers. Record student responses using a concept web.
3. Share that engineers work to develop solutions to problems. They analyze the parts of things like buildings or computers, understand how the parts work, and put them together to build new things. They also figure out how to take things like big buildings apart safely and efficiently. Explain that sometimes unfamiliar words can be a challenge when we read or when we want to write. We may not know how to pronounce a word or spell a word we want to use. We can become word engineers. We can learn about words and word parts, especially big words, and use this knowledge

to build and take apart words, learning how words are similar to or different from one another.

4. Draw a new concept web, and write *word engineer* in the center. Lead students in a discussion of the things word engineers can do (learn word parts, make new words, break down big words, pronounce big or unfamiliar words, spell big words, figure out what words mean, etc.). Have students record this concept web on the first page of their notebooks.

Differentiation

There is great flexibility in the amount of independence students can exercise when using the Word Engineer notebooks throughout the year. The notebooks can be used during whole-class and small-group instruction. Notebooks can be personalized and differentiated to meet students' unique word recognition needs. Some students can collect and record words independently while others will need scaffolded guidance to find and record words outside of lessons that use the notebooks.

Build Words with Prefixes

Objectives

- Know and apply grade-level phonics and word analysis skills when decoding words.

- Use combined knowledge of all letter-sound correspondences, syllabication patterns, and morphology to accurately read unfamiliar multisyllabic words in context and out of context.

Background Information

Morphemic analysis is the process of breaking down a word into parts, such as affixes (prefixes and suffixes), base words, and roots. Explicit instruction in morphemic analysis is an important part of word recognition in the upper elementary grades. When students encounter new, complex words, breaking these words into parts can help them decode, pronounce, and determine the meanings of the words. Morphological awareness is predictive of word reading skills and positively correlated to reading comprehension (Levesque, Kieffer, and Deacon 2017). Build Words with Prefixes develops knowledge of morphology and word parts by having students use prefixes to build new words. This a flexible strategy that can be used to learn word parts and to decode and encode multisyllabic words.

Materials

- Word Engineer notebooks (see page 25; optional)

- list of prefixes and base words

- *Build Words with Prefixes* (page 30)

Process

Note: Use this strategy after introducing the idea of "word engineers" and having students begin using their Word Engineer notebooks (see page 25).

1. Distribute the *Build Words with Prefixes* activity sheets to students, or have them create the chart in their Word Engineer notebooks.

2. Remind students that engineers analyze the parts of things like buildings or computers, understand how the parts work, and put parts together to build new things. Words have different parts too. Word engineers can put word parts together to make different words. Explain that today, we are going to build words. We will put word parts together to make different words.

3. Introduce a list of common prefixes to students (see the appendix for a reference list). This list can be elicited from students if they are familiar with prefixes. Explain that

prefixes are added to the beginning of words, and they change the meaning, but not the spelling, of the base word. You can discuss the meanings of the prefixes in greater depth when word study focuses on meaning making, but in this lesson the primary focus is on encoding and building new words rather than trying to remember the changed definitions of each word.

4. Provide a list of base words, and model how to add prefixes to create new words. Elicit one or two examples from students. Provide time for students to work in pairs to discuss the new words they can create.

5. Elicit new words from students and record them on the list. Have students record the words in their Word Engineer notebooks.

6. Challenge students to find additional words throughout the week that contain the prefixes taught in the lesson. Students can share these findings with you, and the words can be added to a class word chart and/or recorded in their Word Engineer notebooks.

7. This strategy can be used with the whole class or in small groups and can be repeated with a variety of prefixes and base words to introduce and reinforce morphemic analysis skills.

Differentiation

- Some students may benefit from a more tactile experience with word building. The prefixes and base words can be printed in a list or cut up into cards and placed in a sandwich bag. Review the prefixes and base words prior to the lesson. Students can use the list or cards as a reference as the class works to make new words. After the lesson, students can copy the new words into their Word Engineer notebooks. Alternately, they can cut and glue the list/cards into the notebooks.

- Students who demonstrate a strong understanding of prefixes can be encouraged to find their own examples as they read and add these to their notebooks.

Build Words with Prefixes *Example*

prefix un–

base words	new words
happy	<u>un</u>happy
clear	<u>un</u>clear
cover	<u>un</u>cover
pack	<u>un</u>pack
wrap	<u>un</u>wrap
lock	<u>un</u>lock
able	<u>un</u>able
wind	<u>un</u>wind

Name: _____ Date: _____

Build Words with Prefixes

Directions: Write a prefix and base words. Next, build new words by adding the prefix to each base word. Then, see if you can think of other words that use the prefix. Add them to your list.

prefix

base words	new words

Build Words with Suffixes

Objectives

- Know and apply grade-level phonics and word analysis skills when decoding words.
- Use combined knowledge of all letter-sound correspondences, syllabication patterns, and morphology to accurately read unfamiliar multisyllabic words in context and out of context.

Background Information

Making new words with suffixes is more complex than with prefixes since there are multiple types of suffixes that can affect word spellings and meanings. The focus for morphemic analysis in this strategy is decoding and encoding, so it is useful to teach suffix spelling generalizations. In relation to spelling, there are two types of suffixes: vowel suffixes, which begin with a vowel, and consonant suffixes, which begin with a consonant. Once taught, the spelling rules for adding vowel and consonant suffixes should be consistently pointed out and reinforced.

Materials

- Word Engineer notebooks (see page 25; optional)
- list of suffixes and base words
- *Build Words with Suffixes* (page 34)

Process

Note: Use this strategy after introducing the idea of "word engineers" and having students begin using their Word Engineer notebooks (see page 25).

1. Distribute the *Build Words with Suffixes* activity sheets to students, or have them create the chart in their Word Engineer notebooks.

2. Remind students that engineers analyze the parts of things like buildings or computers, understand how the parts work, and put parts together to build new things. Words have different parts too. Word engineers can put word parts together to make new words. Today we are going to build words!

3. Explain that suffixes are affixes that are added to the ends of words. Introduce a list of common suffixes to students (see the appendix for a reference list). This list can be elicited from students if they are familiar with suffixes. Suffixes are used to make new words and can change the spelling of the base word. Identify the suffixes by

the defining feature you have used to group the selected suffixes. If this is the first time you are teaching suffixes, introduce students to the spelling generalizations for suffixes (see the appendix). Make an anchor chart of these generalizations and post it for reference.

4. Provide a list of base words, and model how to add suffixes to create new words. Elicit one or two examples from students. Be explicit about the spelling rules that apply. Provide time for students to work in pairs to discuss the new words they can create.

5. Elicit new words from students and list them. Students may record them in their notebooks.

6. Challenge students to find additional words throughout the week that contain the suffixes taught in the lesson. Students can share these findings with you, and the words can be added to a class word chart and/or recorded in their notebooks.

7. This strategy can be used with the whole class or in small groups and can be repeated with a variety of suffixes and base words to introduce and reinforce morphemic analysis skills.

Differentiation

- Some students may benefit from a more tactile experience with word building. This lesson can be scaffolded for students who need extra support by providing the suffixes and base words that will be used in the lesson. The words can be printed in a list or cut up into cards and placed in a sandwich bag. Students can use the list or cards as a reference as the class works to make new words. Have students copy the new words into their Word Engineer notebooks or cut and glue the list/cards into the notebooks.

- Challenge advanced students to generate additional words using the suffixes.

Build Words with Suffixes *Example*

suffix   -less

base words	new words
care	care<u>less</u>
use	use<u>less</u>
mind	mind<u>less</u>
thank	thank<u>less</u>
pain	pain<u>less</u>
hope	hope<u>less</u>
taste	taste<u>less</u>
fear	fear<u>less</u>
	home<u>less</u>
	end<u>less</u>
	job<u>less</u>
	point<u>less</u>
	help<u>less</u>
	rest<u>less</u>

Build Words with Suffixes

Directions: Write a suffix and base words. Next, build new words by adding the suffix to each base word. Then, see if you can think of other words that use the sufffix. Add them to your list.

suffix

base words	new words

Word Morph

Objectives

- Know and apply grade-level phonics and word analysis skills when decoding words.
- Use combined knowledge of all letter-sound correspondences, syllabication patterns, and morphology to accurately read unfamiliar multisyllabic words in context and out of context.

Background Information

Once students have familiarity with a large bank of affixes, they should engage in activities that strengthen their ability to decode and encode words by morphemes, recognizing the word parts and grouping words that share common base words into word families. Word Morph is a morphemic transformation strategy (Shefelbine and Newman 2004) that provides practice in identifying root words and recognizing the ways affixes affect pronunciation. The teacher-directed portion of this strategy focuses on recognizing affixes and base words to support decoding; students then work together to add affixes to make multisyllabic words, which builds encoding skills. Word Morph is a flexible strategy that can be used with the whole class or in small groups.

Materials

- Word Engineer notebooks (see page 25; optional)
- list of words combining one base word with affixes
- *Word Morph* (page 38)

Process

Note: Use this strategy after introducing the idea of "word engineers" and having students begin using their Word Engineer notebooks (see page 25).

1. Review the meaning of *base word*. A base word is a word to which affixes may be added to create a related word.

2. Choose a list of words combining a base word with affixes, and write the words on the board. The list should be grade-level appropriate. For example, for the base word *depend*, list the following words: *independent, interdependent, dependent, dependency, independence*. Read each word in the list, pointing to the root word, *depend*, and underlining it as you read. Have students repeat the list of words chorally.

3. Explain that you can add prefixes, suffixes, and sometimes both to base words to make bigger words. Sometimes these additions change the way the words are pronounced, but not always.

4. Choose a base word for guided practice. Write the word and add a suffix. Underline the suffix and point it out to students. Read the whole word aloud. If the suffix changes the word's pronunciation, be explicit in explaining this. For example: add *—al* to *nation* to form the word *national*.

5. Erase the suffix and add a different suffix. Underline the suffix and read the word aloud.

6. Explain that we can make even bigger words using both prefixes and suffixes. Demonstrate by adding a prefix and suffix to the same base word. Underline the prefix and the suffix and read the word aloud (for example, *international*).

7. Ask students to generate additional words by adding affixes to the base word. List the words and underline the affix in each one. Explain that the list shows a *word family*. Identifying base words in word families can help us to quickly recognize multisyllabic words.

8. Give students *Word Morph* and a new base word, and have them work in pairs to create new words by adding affixes to the same base. When finished, have partners share the words they made. List them on the board, underlining the affixes and reading the lists. Discuss any changes in pronunciation. Students can compare their lists to the lists of others and add to their notebooks.

Differentiation

Some students may benefit from practice in small groups using different base words. Some students may need lists of common affixes as a scaffold when generating lists of words in the word family. Students with advanced morphology skills may benefit from practice with words that have multiple affixes.

Word Morph *Example*

Base word: friend

My new words:

friendly

friendship

friendliness

unfriend

unfriended

unfriendly

befriend

friends

befriended

Word Morph

Directions: Write a base word. Use your knowledge of prefixes and suffixes to build new words related to the base word. Underline the prefixes and suffixes you add.

Base word: _____

My new words:

_____

_____

_____

_____

_____

_____

_____

_____

_____

_____

_____

_____

_____

_____

_____

_____

_____

Beat the Clock

Objectives

- Know and apply grade-level phonics and word analysis skills when decoding words.
- Use combined knowledge of all letter-sound correspondences, syllabication patterns, and morphology to accurately read unfamiliar multisyllabic words in context and out of context.

Background Information

Beat the Clock (Toste, Williams, and Capin 2016) supports students in reading familiar and unfamiliar multisyllabic words. This strategy gives students the opportunity to use morphemic analysis to decode longer words and supports their growing knowledge of affixes and base words. Beat the Clock encourages students to work quickly, promoting the development of automaticity. This type of strategy is often referred to as a *peel-off strategy* or *peel-off reading*. Peel-off strategies teach students to remove, or peel off, affixes to reveal the base and decode the word. The goal is automaticity and fluency so students eventually expend less effort decoding and can focus on comprehension. This flexible strategy can be used with various words in whole- or small-group settings.

Materials

- *Beat the Clock* (page 42)
- list of multisyllabic words
- stopwatch

Process

1. Give students a list of multisyllabic words such as those on the *Beat the Clock* activity sheet (page 42). Initially the list should include words with prefixes, then words with suffixes, and eventually words with both prefixes and suffixes.
2. Guide students in underlining the affix in each word.
3. Use choral reading to read aloud the underlined affixes. Read only the affix, not the entire word. Make sure students are pronouncing the affixes correctly; provide feedback as necessary.
4. Use choral reading to read the list again, reading each entire word this time. Again, pay attention to pronunciation.

5. Pair students for timed reading. This works best if students have access to a stopwatch. Student partners can use apps on tablets or phones as stopwatches, or teachers can project a digital stopwatch in the classroom. One student reads the list of whole words aloud as their partner follows along with their finger on their own list. Once they have read the complete list, they record their times at the bottom of their *Beat the Clock* activity sheets. Students then switch roles. After each student has read the list one time, they take turns reading the list again, focusing on improving their times (beat the clock!) while maintaining accurate pronunciation.

Differentiation

- Adjust the number and difficulty of words used during the lesson and during additional practice.

- Students may find it helpful to highlight rather than underline affixes to call more attention to them.

- It may be useful for students to fold the lists, revealing only half of the words at a time during the timed reading.

- It may also be useful for students to practice reading these lists multiple times throughout the week to improve their personal best times.

Beat the Clock *Example*

dislike

pretest

telephone

friendly

attention

enjoyment

misbehave

nonsense

exhale

invite

sadness

dentist

happily

catches

baker

enjoyable

1st Read	2nd Read	3rd Read
225 seconds	215 seconds	195 seconds

Beat the Clock

Directions: Underline the prefix or the suffix in each word. Practice reading the list of words with a partner several times to see if you can improve your time!

dislike   exhale

pretest   invite

telephone   sadness

friendly   dentist

attention   happily

enjoyment   catches

misbehave   baker

nonsense   enjoyable

1st Read	2nd Read	3rd Read
_____ seconds	_____ seconds	_____ seconds

  Literacy Strategies—131698

Word Sort

Objectives

- Know and apply grade-level phonics and word analysis skills when decoding words.
- Use combined knowledge of all letter-sound correspondences, syllabication patterns, and morphology to accurately read unfamiliar multisyllabic words in context and out of context.

Background Information

Word Sort (Bear and Barone 1998; Bear et al. 2020) requires readers to categorize words by finding common features, spelling patterns, roots, bases, and so on. This categorization helps readers build their understandings of the patterns and form generalizations that aid in decoding, encoding, and fluency building. Readers later apply these generalizations to unknown words. Bear and Barone (1998) and Bear et al. (2020) describe three types of sorts: sound, pattern, and meaning. Pattern sorts reinforce morphological analysis skills for upper elementary readers. Words can be sorted by common affixes, base words, and suffix spelling generalizations. Word sorts can be closed or open. In a closed sort, the teacher defines the sorting criteria (e.g., labeling the sort with specific prefix or suffix headings). In open sorts, students analyze the list of words to identify commonalities and then create the categories themselves.

Materials

- list of words to be sorted
- sentence strips or cards (optional)

Process

1. Develop a list of words that share the focus and distinction of the Word Sort. For example, if the focus is on making words plural, develop a list including examples of words that become plural by adding –s and others that become plural by adding –es.

2. Introduce the list of words to students. Read the words aloud, paying special attention to words that may be unfamiliar or difficult to pronounce.

3. Chorally read the words with students.

4. Conduct a think-aloud to establish the categories for sorting. Model asking questions such as "What do I notice about these words?" or "What do some of these words have in common?" Alternately, as students become familiar with Word Sorts, invite them to generate the categories rather than conducting a think-aloud.

5. Write the categories for the Word Sort on the board.

6. Model sorting several words, checking for student understanding of the sorting criteria. Have students work individually or with partners to sort the rest of the words.

7. Bring students back together to review the sorts. Reflect on the categories and what the words have in common. Reinforce the generalizations by paying attention to the categories and asking questions that allow students to verbalize their understanding.

Differentiation

- Most students in upper elementary grades can write the words directly in their Word Engineer or word study notebooks. However, you can also give students the words in card format for them to physically sort. Students can glue the word cards onto a sheet of paper or later record the words in their notebooks. Preview these cards or lists before the lesson if necessary.

- Word Sorts can be made easier or more difficult for small-group instruction. The number of categories can be increased or decreased, the contrast of the criteria can be made easier or more difficult, and the words chosen for the sort can be more or less complex depending on the number of affixes, lengths, morphemes, and the balance of familiar and unfamiliar words.

- Word sorting by the focus criteria can be reinforced throughout the week by conducting "word hunts." Encourage students to record words that match the criteria from their textbooks, library books, and other reading material. They can also be encouraged to record words they hear in discussions or encounter in media. At the end of the week, place students in groups or pairs to share the words they found during the week.

Examples

Closed Sort

Teach the rules of adding *–s* or *–es* to make certain words plural (for nouns that end in *ch*, *x*, *s*, *z*, or *s*-like sounds, add *–es*). Give students a list of words and have them sort them by their suffixes and explain the rule.

Sample word list: glasses, pencils, lunches, cats, bunches, lamps, boxes, bikes, inches, houses, taxes, plants

–s	–es
pencils	glasses
cats	lunches
lamps	bunches
bikes	boxes
houses	inches
plants	taxes

Open Sort

Teach the generalization for vowel digraphs (the first vowel in the pair is the long vowel sound). Give students a list of words that contain different vowel digraphs that represent the long *e* sound. Have them read each word, discuss the pattern, and sort by the digraph.

Sample word list: sheet, cheat, feet, neat, sheep, peek, speak, read, weak, week, meet, beach, fleet, peach

–ee	–ea
sheet	cheat
feet	neat
sheep	speak
peek	read
week	weak
meet	beach
fleet	peach

Word Break

Objectives

- Know and apply grade-level phonics and word analysis skills in decoding words.
- Decode multisyllabic words.
- Use combined knowledge of all letter-sound correspondences, syllabication patterns, and morphology (e.g., roots and affixes) to accurately read unfamiliar multisyllabic words in context and out of context.

Background Information

Word Break is a strategy readers can use to tackle unfamiliar multisyllabic words. Knowledge of multiple strategies prevents guessing and skipping words and supports accurate, fluent reading. While morphological analysis strategies such as the ones presented previously are helpful, not every word contains prefixes, suffixes, or base words that are familiar to students. In these instances, it is useful for students to be familiar with different syllable types or patterns. This assists students in segmenting a word into its syllables and then blending the syllables to pronounce the word. Segmenting syllables helps students encode as well. Thinking about or listening for vowel sounds in a syllable can help students "map" the phonemes in that syllable onto the letters they write.

Materials

- Word Engineer notebooks
- Syllable Rules Anchor Chart (created by teacher)
- *Syllable Rules Guide* (page 49)

Process

1. Review the types of syllables and how they typically are divided. Display an anchor chart students can reference (see page 48).

2. Choose words from a text the class is currently reading or from a grade-appropriate multisyllabic word list.

3. Think aloud to model how to use the syllabication division patterns to segment a word into its syllables.

4. Choose words for guided practice. Have students write the words on whiteboards or paper and break them apart using dots or slashes to represent the segmentation.

5. Demonstrate blending the syllables together to read the word aloud.

6. Provide the *Syllable Rules Guide*, and work together as a class to have students draw slashes showing where the words should be segmented. Have students glue the guides into their Word Engineer notebooks. Alternately, they can make the guides into flip books and keep them with their notebooks.

7. Pair students and have them practice segmenting words by syllables. Have them share the syllable division patterns they used.

8. Bring the students back together, and have pairs share examples.

Differentiation

During small-group instruction, reinforce this strategy and apply it to words of varying complexity to meet the needs of learners. For some students, it may be useful to introduce syllabication patterns one at a time and reinforce them through practice. Students who are ready can be challenged with longer, more complex multisyllabic words.

Example

Word Break
1) va|ca|tion = 3
2) car|ry = 2
3) fa|ther = 2
4) be|low = 2
5) com|mon = 2
6) dis|miss = 2
7) un|der|stand = 3
8) pho|to = 2
9) no|thing = 2
10) some|thing = 2

Syllable Rules Anchor Chart

1. Divide syllables after a prefix.
   re|wind

2. Divide syllables before a suffix.
   kind|ness

3. Divide between two same consonants.
   let|ter

4. Divide between two middle consonants.
   bas|ket

5. Is there a consonant and vowel in the middle?

   a. Short vowel: Divide after the consonant.
      riv|er

   b. Long vowel: Divide before the consonant.
      ba|by

6. Divide compound words between the words.
   sun|shine

7. Divide consonant -le by word chunks.
   rum|ble

*blends stay together
   bl, sl, fr, br, tr, cl, etc.

*digraphs stay together
   ch, sh, wh, th, kn, ph, etc.

Name: _____ Date: _____

Syllable Rules Guide

Directions: Use the syllable rules to break the words apart. Keep this guide as a reference.

Divide syllables after a prefix. **rewind**	Divide syllables before a suffix. **kindness**
Divide between two same consonants. **letter**	Divide between two middle consonants. **basket**
Consonant and short vowel? Divide after consonant. **river**	Consonant and long vowel? Divide before consonant. **baby**
Divide compound words between the words. **sunshine**	Divide consonant-*le* by word chunks. **rumble**

Phrased Reading

Objective

- Read with accuracy and fluency to support comprehension.

Background Information

Phrased Reading (Rasinski, Yildirim, and Nageldinger 2011) is a fluency strategy to develop prosody and support comprehension. Fluent readers read aloud with expression and intonation, while disfluent readers often struggle to phrase or break text into meaningful "chunks" while they read, instead reading word for word without expression. The ability to "chunk" text into syntactically appropriate and meaningful units helps students read with expression and construct meaning from the text. Phrased Reading makes these chunks visible by marking phrases in a text, explaining the reasoning for the markings, and providing time for students to practice reading. Phrased Reading incorporates several best practices for fluency instruction, including modeling fluent reading, assisted reading (choral reading), and repeated reading. Dedicating 10 to 15 minutes for Phrased Reading several days per week is an effective way to support fluency development.

Materials

- copies of a short text passage for students

Process

1. Prepare for the lesson by selecting a short passage from a text familiar to students—a text they have read, a poem, or a rhyme. A text that lends itself to expressive oral reading is best. Make a copy of the text, and mark appropriate phrase boundaries (where readers would pause) with one slash mark (/) for short phrases and pauses, and two slash marks for the longer pauses between sentences (//).

   Example of Phrased Text Mark-Up

   The Tale of Peter Rabbit

   An old mouse was running in and out over the stone doorstep / carrying peas and beans to her family in the wood. // Peter asked her the way to the gate, / but she had such a large pea in her mouth that she could not answer. // She only shook her head at him. // Peter began to cry.

2. Distribute a copy of the marked-up text to each student. Read it aloud to the class. Direct students to follow along silently. Provide extra emphasis in places where you marked the phrasing.

3. Discuss the passage as a class. Ask students to explain how you were able to convey meaning through your phrasing. Have them consider how you used your voice and pauses to indicate the phrases as you read aloud.

4. Chorally read the passage with your students, again placing emphasis on the marked phrasing. Then give students an opportunity to read the text on their own in low voices or to partners taking turns with one student reading and the other following along silently.

5. Have a few students read the passage as a performance for the other students individually, in pairs, or in small groups.

6. The next day or later in the week, provide students with an unmarked passage (the same one or a similar one) and repeat the routine. After you read the text aloud, emphasizing phrasing, lead the class in a discussion about phrase boundaries and where to mark the text. Once the text is marked, continue with the lesson described above.

Differentiation

Phrased Reading can be implemented in small groups to ensure that students are engaging with texts appropriate for their reading levels. Students at various reading levels will benefit from fluency instruction such as Phrased Reading. Provide students with opportunities to listen to recorded examples of the text as they work to develop their skills with phrasing. Allow students to record themselves and listen to their phrasing to self-evaluate and hear where they might improve.

SECTION II
Reading Comprehension and Content Knowledge

The strategies in this section correspond with key competencies identified in *What the Science of Reading Says about Reading Comprehension and Content Knowledge* (Jump and Kopp 2023). These research-based instructional strategies will help teachers bridge the gap between the science of literacy instruction and classroom practice.

Strategy	Skills and Understandings Addressed					
	Building Content Knowledge	All About Vocabulary	Literacy Knowledge: Print Concepts to Genre Study	Language Structures: Syntax and Semantics	Text Structures and Verbal Reasoning	Reading Comprehension Strategies
Cheat Sheet	■					
Three Key Facts	■					
Anticipation Guide	■					
Talking Drawings	■					
Vocabulary Knowledge Rating		■				
Meaning Morphs		■				
Word Spokes		■				
Interactive Word Walls		■				
Bricks and Mortar		■				
Genre Study			■			

Strategy	Skills and Understandings Addressed (cont.)					
	Building Content Knowledge	All About Vocabulary	Literacy Knowledge: Print Concepts to Genre Study	Language Structures: Syntax and Semantics	Text Structures and Verbal Reasoning	Reading Comprehension Strategies
Sentence Anagrams				■		
Signal Sleuths					■	
Magnet Words					■	
Concept Mapping					■	
Facts-Questions-Responses (FQR)					■	
Rank-Ordering Retell (ROR)						■
One-Sentence Paraphrase						■
Question Journal						■
Annotate and Compare						■

Reading Comprehension and Content Knowledge

Simply put, reading comprehension is understanding what we read. It is the knowledge that words represent thoughts and ideas. It is the skill required for meaning-making, and meaning-making is the very heart of reading. Why read words if we cannot make meaning from them? While we may be able to define reading comprehension simply, the act is not so simple. Researchers from a variety of disciplines have attempted to describe, visualize, theorize, and model the processes that occur in a reader's mind when making meaning from words, and while there may not be a definitive model, there is much we have learned that has significant implications for instructional practices.

In order to comprehend what they read, readers must have strong foundational skills. They must have the ability to accurately and effortlessly decode most or all of the words in a text (Duke, Ward, and Pearson 2021). We know that readers must be able to cognitively process the words, drawing meaning from their own experiences and knowledge to understand the author's message. Many agree that reading is a dialogue between the reader and the author, and during this dialogue, the reader generates questions to help anticipate meaning, search for information, respond intellectually and emotionally, and infer ideas from and explain further the content of the text.

> Readers must be able to cognitively process the words, drawing meaning from their own experiences and knowledge to understand the author's message.

While decoding and fluency skills are necessary components for reading comprehension, it is widely accepted that they are not sufficient. In the upper elementary grades, reading comprehension instruction should provide a bridge between readers' foundational skills, namely decoding and fluency skills, and comprehension. As discussed in the word recognition section, students in grades 3 through 5 engage with increasingly complex text in terms of the lexical complexity of words and of the thoughts, ideas, and information expressed in text. Appropriate instruction is designed in ways that support the development of the skills for and the transition to independent reading during the upper elementary years.

Academic Vocabulary and Morphology

An abundance of research has demonstrated the critical role of vocabulary knowledge in reading comprehension (Cromley and Azevedo 2007; Perfetti and Stafura 2013). So much so that researchers have referred to vocabulary knowledge as the "central connection point" between a reader's word recognition knowledge and their comprehension of text (Perfetti and Stafura 2013, 24). The meanings of many of the increasingly complex words students encounter hold the key to understanding the information and ideas expressed by the author.

As readers grow older, they must develop increasingly sophisticated and robust academic vocabularies. Academic vocabulary has two components: (1) domain-specific academic vocabulary, and (2) general academic vocabulary. Domain-specific academic vocabulary is what most of us likely consider academic vocabulary; these are low-frequency words, mostly confined to use in a specific discipline like math, or science, or history (Baumann and Graves 2010). Teachers may be familiar with the terms "tier 3 words" (Beck, McKeown, and Kucan 2002) or "technical vocabulary" (Fisher and Frey 2008) to describe domain-specific academic vocabulary. Think words such as *acronym, isosceles,* or *osmosis.* This is the vocabulary one needs to learn conceptual ideas and subject-matter information.

In contrast, general academic vocabulary consists of words that are used across disciplines to explain, describe, and connect ideas and thoughts. These words are what many might consider markers of a sophisticated vocabulary or the language of school, sometimes referred to as "tier 2 words" (Beck, McKeown, and Kucan 2002). Think words such as *recognize, support,* and *include.* These more frequently occurring words are often parts of larger word families (*support, supported, unsupportive*); therefore, derivational and morphological knowledge are important for readers to acquire.

> Developing a more robust oral and written vocabulary and the skills to tackle unknown words will accelerate comprehension as students encounter increasingly complex academic and literary texts.

Vocabulary development should be considered a vital part of comprehension instruction. Suggested instruction includes (1) explicit vocabulary instruction focused on definitions and morphological analysis; (2) repeated exposures to new words; (3) multiple exposures to new words through authentic activities like speaking, listening, and writing; and (4) the learning of strategies to determine the meaning of unknown words independently. Developing a more robust oral and written vocabulary and the skills to tackle unknown words will accelerate comprehension as students encounter increasingly complex academic and literary texts (Kamil et al. 2008).

Syntax and Semantics

An understanding of how language structure works, through the development of syntactical and semantic knowledge, aids reading comprehension. Syntax is the system of how words are arranged to make sense in a language. *Syntactical knowledge* includes an understanding of the functions of words and the rules of grammar that govern word arrangement, impacting and conveying meaning in a sentence. *Semantics* refers to the overall meaning of a sentence or the message the words convey. An essential part of semantic knowledge involves knowing how to determine the differences between words that convey similar meanings and understanding how these differences affect meaning, for example, knowing how the use of the word *jog* as opposed to *run* changes the meaning of the sentence. This grasp of the structure of language helps readers process and understand text at the sentence level. While vocabulary development facilitates the comprehension of individual words, knowledge of language structure helps readers figure out how the arrangement of words in a sentence influences the meaning. Instructional activities that focus students' attention to the sentence level, attending to the ways words, clauses, and phrases combine to make meaning are effective in developing knowledge of language structure (LeVasseur, Macaruso, and Shankweiler 2008).

Reading Comprehension Strategies

Decades of research have helped us determine what effective readers do as they read (NRP 2000). Some of the most interesting findings came from the work of Pressley and Afflerbach (1995), in which proficient readers explained what was happening in their minds while reading by thinking aloud to the researchers. From this and other studies, we have learned that good readers have pre-reading behaviors that include setting a purpose for reading and previewing text to take note of organizational patterns and text structure. Proficient readers draw from their prior knowledge to predict events and information, generate hypotheses as they read, and determine the meaning of unknown words or confusing phrases. They make inferences, make connections between ideas and texts, draw conclusions, and summarize. These readers ask themselves questions throughout the reading process. If we wanted to summarize these behaviors into one sentence, we would be correct in stating that *proficient readers are strategic readers.*

> Reading comprehension strategies have been defined as cognitive and metacognitive processes that readers use deliberately and consciously for the means of understanding what they are reading.

It stands to reason that upper elementary teachers can develop better readers by providing strategy instruction to model and scaffold behaviors of strategic reading. Reading comprehension strategies have been defined as cognitive and metacognitive processes that readers use deliberately and consciously for the means of understanding what they are reading (Almasi and Hart 2018; Paris, Lipson, and Wixson 1983; Pressley, Borkowski, and Schneider 1987). According to Shanahan, "Strategies like monitoring, self-questioning, visualizing, comparing the text with prior knowledge, identifying text organization, and so on are all intentional, purposeful actions that are effective in improving comprehension or recall" (2018, para. 7). Teaching the following strategies to students has been shown to increase reading comprehension: activating background knowledge, making predictions, making inferences, visualizing, identifying text organization, generating questions, summarizing, and monitoring comprehension (Shanahan et al. 2010). Strategy instruction is a key part of teaching reading in the upper elementary grades. However, it is important to note that strategy instruction is just *one* component of reading comprehension instruction, and research does not recommend strategies to be taught in isolation. We teach strategies because we have learned they represent what good readers do when they read—they are strategic readers. Therefore, strategy instruction is not meant to teach readers to use a strategy but to teach them to be strategic. Almasi and Hart describe why this distinction is important: "The difference [between teaching students a 'strategy' versus teaching students to be 'strategic'] is that strategic actions require intentionality—they require a reader who is actively processing the text and making decisions about it" (2018, 228). Instruction that scaffolds students' selection of appropriate strategies, embeds strategy instruction, and involves multiple strategies is most effective.

Content Knowledge

Since the ultimate goal of our instruction is to produce competent, independent, strategic readers, we must address the needs of the whole reader and develop their capacities to know not just how but when to use strategies. Several of the strategies referenced above rely on the reader activating and making connections to their background knowledge. Decades of reading research have shown that along with decoding and fluency skills, another key to reading comprehension is the development of a broad base of knowledge one can activate and apply to the reading situation. This knowledge includes topics we covered previously such as academic vocabulary, morphology, and familiarity with text and language structures, but it also includes topical knowledge. Wattenberg points out that "as students age and gain basic skills, the lack of knowledge typically becomes the much greater obstacle to good reading" (2016, 2).

In the upper elementary grades, students continue to engage with a wide range of informational texts. A broad base of content or topical knowledge can give readers a comprehension advantage when they encounter a diversity of topics, particularly in science and social studies. Research demonstrates that having schema (relevant prior knowledge) for a topic aids not only in the comprehension process, but also in the learning process (Anderson and Nagy 1992; Anderson and Pearson 1984; Kintsch 1988). When a topic or concept is introduced in text and students can initiate the retrieval process (activating their schema for the topic), they have an anchor to which they can connect the new information to better understand it (Anderson and Pearson 1984). Think of our schema as a set of folders in a filing cabinet (or in our "cloud storage"): it is easier for us to add items to our existing folders than it is to create a whole new folder with a whole new label and find things to fill it with. This is an overly simplistic but helpful analogy for thinking about the importance of schema. The advantage this broad knowledge bestows goes beyond the facts and information of a topic. When students have knowledge of facts, ideas, and concepts across content areas, they can develop an understanding of how concepts/topics are related, how they are explained, how processes work, and more. This familiarity can be transferred to new topics and content to facilitate learning.

Content and concept knowledge can support incidental word learning. When students have knowledge of a concept or topic, that information allows them to better understand new vocabulary or technical vocabulary related to that concept. This knowledge of related words can activate broader semantic networks (the organization of facts and knowledge in the mind) to enhance comprehension and accelerate new learning (Cervetti, Wright, and Hwang 2016; Willingham 2006). Content and concept knowledge will also assist readers in understanding words with multiple meanings. For example, exposure to and broad knowledge of marine life can help a reader distinguish the differing meanings of the word *school*, as in a *school of fish* as opposed to an *elementary school*. Similarly, familiarity with a topic can help students understand figurative language, distinguish that a statement is indeed figurative and not literal, and interpret the meaning of the figurative statement. For example, students read that a team of scientists really "hit it out of the park" with the results of their latest study. Exposure to or familiarity with baseball would help these students understand (1) that this is a figurative statement—that the scientists did not actually hit anything, and an actual park was not involved—and (2) that their results were significant and considered remarkable.

> When students have knowledge of facts, ideas, and concepts across content areas, they can develop an understanding of how concepts/topics are related, how they are explained, how processes work, and more.

The recommendations for supporting content learning are related to those for teaching reading comprehension. It is not possible that we could teach students all of the facts, information, and concepts they are likely to encounter in every piece of text! Therefore, isolated instruction is not beneficial. Embedded strategy instruction is the key. Embedding this instruction in a wide variety of text genres and providing exposure to multiple texts develops layers and depth of knowledge. The recognition of the importance of building a broad base of content knowledge is part of the push to increase the amount of informational text students engage with during elementary school. Informational text also allows for instruction in different genres and text structures, furthering students' knowledge of organizational patterns, language structures, and knowledge across domains.

The strategies in this chapter are intended to develop competent, independent, strategic readers who can understand and learn from a diversity of texts across a wide variety of topics. This type of reader can flexibly and independently employ various strategies when reading, making decisions about which strategies to use and switching between strategies when necessary. Great teachers know that some strategies work for some students and other strategies work for other students, just as some strategies work best with certain types of reading material. The most important thing to remember when trying to improve reading comprehension in students is that the skill level, group dynamic, and makeup of students should determine the approach to take and which modifications to lessons may be needed.

The recognition of the importance of building a broad base of content knowledge is part of the push to increase the amount of informational text students engage with during elementary school.

Cheat Sheet

Objectives

- Determine the main idea of sources including texts, digital texts, and other multimedia resources; recount the key details and explain how they support the main idea.
- Use information gained from illustrations (e.g., maps, photographs) and the words in a text to demonstrate understanding of the topic or concept.

Background Information

Cheat Sheet is a strategy to support students in building knowledge of a topic before, during, and after reading. Prior knowledge of a topic is a critical factor in reading comprehension (Wexler 2019). Many strategies rely on activating prior knowledge, but sometimes students come to a topic with very limited background. Research demonstrates that teaching words in categories, engaging students in topic-focused wide reading, and incorporating multimedia are effective strategies for building knowledge (Neuman, Kaefer, and Pinkham 2014). Cheat Sheet includes and builds on all three of these practices. This strategy can be used over several lessons or an entire unit, and it can be used to support a particularly complex text.

Materials

- *Cheat Sheet* (page 63)
- multimedia resources on topic of study

Process

1. Create a *Cheat Sheet* to introduce a topic using the template (page 63). The *Cheat Sheet* can include background information, links to video examples, support pictures, important quotes, defined vocabulary, vocabulary to look for, considerations, additional texts to read, questions, and sentence frames.

2. Give each student a *Cheat Sheet*. Introduce the topic and explain the purpose of the *Cheat Sheet*: It provides background information, things to know, and things to wonder about, and it supports you as you learn about this topic (or read this text). The *Cheat Sheet* is designed to help you access the important information in this unit (or text).

3. Discuss the information on the *Cheat Sheet*. Allow students time to review the sheet and the provided resources independently before engaging in the content learning activities.

4. Encourage students to use the back of the sheet to take notes as they read and view the background materials. After engaging with these resources, students should be able to write a brief summary explaining the topic, define some or most of the key vocabulary, and answer some of the questions in the last section of the sheet.

5. Review or discuss what students learned from the resources. Have students share with classmates their definitions, summaries, and answers to questions.

6. Explain to students they will continue to use the *Cheat Sheet* to record ideas and details throughout the study of the topic.

Differentiation

- Provide additional support during small-group instruction by explaining challenging topics, defining vocabulary, and using the sentence stems. It may also be beneficial for some students to work on the *Cheat Sheet* with partners.

- As students become more skilled in using the *Cheat Sheet* as a knowledge-building strategy, you may wish to have students write some of their own questions, use the stems as starters for small-group discussions, expand their summaries, or find additional resources to share with their classmates.

- Provide the *Cheat Sheet* in a digital format, giving students easier access to digital content to support the building of background knowledge and learning connections.

Cheat Sheet *Example*

Topic: Heroes who took risks: Harriet Tubman

General Background

- Look at the <u>map</u> to help you understand the United States during the time of the Underground Railroad.
- Check out these <u>images of Harriet Tubman</u>.
- Watch this <u>video clip</u>.
- Define the terms in the glossary.

Things to Consider

- What important information are you learning? What questions do you have?
- What connections are you making to what you already knew?

Topic: <u>Harriet Tubman</u>

Harriet Tubman was an enslaved woman who escaped and then helped many others escape slavery through the Underground Railroad. **Harriet Tubman** fought for freedom and rights for enslaved people and women.

Glossary

abolitionist—

conductor—

passenger—

station—

Sentence Stems and Questions

1. Harriet Tubman was the most famous _____ on the Underground Railroad.
2. What was the Underground Railroad?
3. When did Harriet Tubman take "passengers" on the Underground Railroad? Why?
4. What did Harriet Tubman do during the Civil War?
5. At the end of her life, what did Harriet Tubman fight for?

Name: _____ Date: _____

Cheat Sheet

Directions: View the resources. Record what you learn. Use the back of this paper to write additional notes as you learn interesting facts and ideas.

Topic: _____

General Background

Things to Consider

Topic: _____

Glossary

Sentence Stems and Questions

Three Key Facts

Objectives

- Determine the main idea of sources including texts, digital texts, and other multimedia resources; recount the key details and explain how they support the main idea.

- Use information gained from a variety of sources to demonstrate understanding of the topic or concept.

Background Information

Three Key Facts builds background knowledge by using multimedia resources. Background knowledge plays a vital role in reading comprehension, listening comprehension, and continued learning of more complex concepts and ideas. In addition to detailed concept knowledge, students need broad knowledge of a variety of topics, ideas, and concepts to allow them to read material aimed at a "general audience" (Hirsch 2006). Creators of content rely on the notion that their readers or viewers bring with them some relevant background knowledge they can apply to understand the material. Yet teachers cannot teach every conceivable topic students need to have a broad base of background knowledge. This strategy helps students gain broad understanding of topics by viewing informational videos and focusing on key facts. Today's students are avid consumers of video, and this strategy gives them a framework for purposefully engaging with such resources in their lives outside of school.

Materials

- Three Key Facts activity sheet (created by teacher)
- short video clip on topic of study

Process

1. Select a video clip on a relevant topic. Ideally the clip will be more than two minutes but less than five minutes. Short videos help students more easily identify key information.

2. Develop a prompt that focuses students on the type of information they need to find. For example, if students are watching a short video related to communities and transportation, you might prompt them to identify three forms of transportation.

Example: *As you watch this short video about communities and transportation, find three ways you can get from here to there (three forms of transportation).*

Create a Three Key Facts activity sheet that includes the prompt.

3. Provide students with the activity sheet. Explain that they are going to watch the video, listen for three key facts, and record the facts on the activity sheet. Tell students that these three facts are "key takeaways." They are broad, major ideas related to a topic rather than discrete details or facts.

4. Show the video and have students record their facts. When finished, have students share with partners or small groups. Then discuss the key facts as a whole class.

5. Provide students the opportunity to use this background knowledge multiple times through reading relevant texts, in their writing, or by engaging in extended learning on a related topic.

Differentiation

Scaffold the process as needed by providing sentence stems or suggested vocabulary to accompany the activity sheet. When watching the video, pause at select points, and have students partner with one another to identify and discuss important information.

Anticipation Guide

Objectives

- Cite textual evidence to support analysis of what the text says explicitly as well as inferences drawn from the text.

- Determine a central idea of a text and how it is conveyed through particular details; provide a summary of the text distinct from personal opinions or judgments.

- Analyze in detail how a key individual, event, or idea is introduced, illustrated, and elaborated in a text.

Background Information

Anticipation guides increase interest, develop motivation, and engage students. They encourage students to express opinions, make connections to prior knowledge, and make predictions about the topic they will study. This variation incorporates multimedia resources such as websites and video or audio clips and focuses students on engaging with the content rather than being passive observers. Using multimedia resources supports building background knowledge by both activating knowledge students may have and frontloading information for students with limited or surface knowledge of a topic. Students first take a position on several statements. They engage with multimedia and then respond to the statements again, using their new knowledge to support their responses. Anticipation guides help set a purpose for engaging with multimedia as students view or listen to find information that supports or challenges their positions.

Materials

- anticipation guide (created by teacher)
- multimedia resource on topic of study

Process

1. Identify a multimedia resource related to the topic of study, and preview it to determine important concepts students should focus on. Prepare an anticipation guide of several short statements about these concepts or ideas (see examples below). The statements should be designed to activate prior knowledge students may have about the topic. True/false or agree/disagree statements work best. Present the statements in the order in which the ideas appear in the resource.

2. Distribute the anticipation guide to students before they engage with the multimedia selection, and allow time for students to read the statements and respond in the "Before" column.

3. Hold a class discussion, asking students to share their responses.

4. Have students engage with the multimedia selection as a class, individually, or with partners as appropriate. Tell students they should look or listen for evidence that supports or refutes their "Before" responses. Have students complete the "After" column on the guide as they discover evidence.

5. Engage in a collaborative discussion about the "After" answers, asking students to explain their thinking. Ask students if they changed their responses as a result of the multimedia resource.

Differentiation

- With new or particularly challenging topics, you may wish to scaffold learning by preparing stopping points in the multimedia resource, guiding students step by step through the content in smaller chunks. Alternately, students can work in groups to respond to the anticipation guide after they engage with the resource.

- This activity can be extended by having students write about whether their new learning supports their "Before" opinions, citing evidence from the resource. Students should be allowed to disagree with information they heard if they can successfully create an argument and support it with details.

Examples

True/False Anticipation Guide

Before		Statement	After	
T	F		T	F
		Coal, oil, and gas are fossil fuels. Evidence:		
		Fossil fuels are burned to make energy. Evidence:		
		Fossil fuels are the only way to make energy. Evidence:		

Agree/Disagree Anticipation Guide

Before		Statement	After	
A	D		A	D
		It is important to ride a bike that is the right size for you. Evidence:		
		Kids should always wear bike helmets. Evidence:		
		Kids also need to wear helmets when they ride their scooters or skate. Evidence:		
		If you are a good bike rider, you don't need your helmet. Evidence:		
		It doesn't matter which side of the road you ride your bike on. Evidence:		

Talking Drawings

Objectives

- Activate prior knowledge related to the information and events in texts.
- Integrate information from text.

Background Information

Talking Drawings (Cappello and Walker 2021) helps students access prior knowledge and integrate new learning with this prior knowledge. Advanced comprehension requires readers to be able to do this (Cabell and Hwang 2020). When this integration occurs, readers deepen their knowledge of a topic (Kintsch 2018). Talking Drawings assists in making this process explicit. Used before reading informational text, this strategy taps existing schema by having students recall and draw any information they may already know related to a topic. After reading, students create new drawings that incorporate details, ideas, and concepts they learned. Students then write a comparison of the two drawings. This last step allows students to assess their prior knowledge and explain their newly acquired knowledge, helping them make explicit connections between their existing knowledge and the new information they learned.

Materials

- *Talking Drawings* (page 72)
- text or multimedia resources on topic of study

Process

1. Tell students the topic of the lesson. Distribute *Talking Drawings* to students. Have students fold the activity sheets.

2. Direct students to close their eyes and visualize the topic. While their eyes are closed, prompt them to visualize everything they know about the topic (*who, what, where, when,* and *how* prompts may be useful, depending on the topic).

3. Tell students to open their eyes, and have them draw what they saw in their minds in section 1 of the activity sheet.

4. Have students discuss their drawings with partners. Remind students to share details about their drawings with their partners but not to add anything to their own drawings during this time. This is an active listening activity.

5. Engage students in new learning about the topic. This can be through reading a text, engaging with multimedia resources, and so on.

6. Have students create a drawing in section 2 of the activity sheet. Remind students to draw a new drawing rather than revise their original. Prompt students to include new information and details they learned. Give students time to discuss their new drawings with their partners.

7. Prompt students to reflect on the similarities and differences between their two drawings. Have students write a description of these in section 3 on the activity sheet. Then debrief as a class.

Differentiation

Students who need additional support may benefit from the use of sentence frames to guide the partner discussions and sentence or paragraph frames to support their comparison writing in section 3. Students may also benefit from adding labels or captions to their drawings to help them incorporate their knowledge and organize their thinking. Encourage students who have a depth of prior knowledge on the topic to write questions about what they may still want to learn and explore those questions.

Talking Drawings *Example*

1. Close your eyes and think about the topic. Open your eyes and draw everything you saw in your mind.

2. Create a new drawing that adds details about what you have learned.

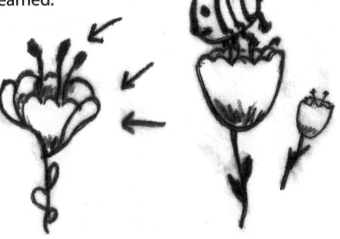

3. Describe the differences between your first drawing and your second drawing, and explain why you made these changes.

In the first drawing I drew the bee near the flower because I know that bees like flowers. In my new drawing the bee is in the flower gathering pollen on its legs from the anthers of the flower. The bee will take this pollen to another flower to pollinate it.

Name: _____ Date: _____

Talking Drawings

Directions: Fold along the dotted lines. Complete each section when your teacher tells you to do so.

1. Close your eyes and think about the topic. Open your eyes and draw everything you saw in your mind.

- -

2. Create a new drawing that adds details about what you have learned.

- -

3. Describe the differences between your first drawing and your second drawing, and explain why you made these changes.

_____

_____

_____

_____

_____

Vocabulary Knowledge Rating

Objective

- Determine the meaning of general academic and domain-specific words or phrases in grade-level text.

Background Information

Vocabulary Knowledge Rating (Blachowicz and Fisher 2006) is a strategy that allows students to rate their knowledge of target vocabulary words before reading and later evaluate their word learning after reading. Rating words prior to reading can promote word consciousness by helping students think about words and be aware of them as they read. By identifying terms students do not know well, teachers are better prepared to support student learning of the topic or concept. After reading, and after discussing the words, students revisit their ratings to reflect on their enhanced or new understandings. This strategy encourages students to think metacognitively about their understanding of each word and the related concepts. It also promotes the independent acquisition of new vocabulary.

Materials

- *Vocabulary Knowledge Rating* (page 76)
- text selection

Process

1. Prior to assigning a reading selection, choose the most essential words in the lesson or unit, making sure to include words that may be unknown to students. Write the selected words on *Vocabulary Knowledge Rating* and make student copies.

2. Distribute *Vocabulary Knowledge Rating* to students, and explain that they will be thinking about their understanding of the words before reading, during reading, and after reading and discussing the words with the class.

3. Explain the rating values: (+) indicates students know the word well; (–) indicates students do not know the word; and (?) indicates students have heard of the word but are not sure of its meaning.

4. Ask students to read the words silently and rate the words in the Before Reading column. If they know a word well, they can write the definition in their own words. As they read the text, students should note where they find the unknown words by recording the page number or paragraph. If they can determine a word's definition, tell them to jot it down. If not, they can continue reading and return to the word when they have finished reading the text selection.

5. After students have read the text, place them in small groups, or hold a class discussion, in which students share which words they knew before reading, which words they were able to figure out during reading, and what they think the words mean. Clarify any words they still do not know. Have students evaluate their knowledge by rating the words again.

Differentiation

For students who may need more support, recite the words on the list or have students recite them before conducting their initial ratings. For some students it may be helpful to include known forms of the target words (for example: *magnet* for *magnetism*), so they can build on their prior knowledge. Differentiate the lists by adjusting the number or level of the words assigned, either to scaffold students' reading and vocabulary development or to encourage independent word exploration for students who are ready.

Vocabulary Knowledge Rating *Example*

Before Reading		During Reading	After Reading	
Word	Rating	Page/ Paragraph	Write a definition. Add an example of how it is used in the text.	New Rating
annual	?	p. 1	Annual means it happens every year The annual migration of the butterflies...	+
disclose	?	p. 1	Disclose means to tell people It was very important they did not disclose their location.	?
queasy	–	p. 2	Queasy means when your stomach hurts like you might throw up The waiting was making Maya queasy with anticipation.	+
sole	+	p. 3	Sole can mean the only one or all alone. I know it can also be the bottom part of a shoe. And finally, a sole Monarch appeared on the horizon...	+

Vocabulary Knowledge Rating

Directions: Rate each word using the key. During reading, write the page number the word first appears on. Write the definition. Add examples from the text.

+ I know the word well.

− I do not know the word.

? I have heard of the word but I'm not sure of its meaning.

Before Reading		During Reading	After Reading	
Word	Rating	Page/ Paragraph	Write a definition. Add an example of how it is used in the text.	New Rating

Meaning Morphs

Objectives

- Determine the meaning of general academic and domain-specific words or phrases as they are used in grade-level text.

- Use common, grade-appropriate Greek and Latin affixes and bases as clues to the meaning of a word.

Background Information

Meaning Morphs complement Word Morphs (page 35), extending students' application of morphology to meaning making. As students become more advanced readers, they acquire a large knowledge store of prefixes, suffixes, and bases. Using this to build vocabulary knowledge is highly effective. The *Meaning Morphs* chart is a fantastic way for students to learn individual words. They can add it to their Word Engineer notebooks (page 25) and use it to collect words they learn throughout the year. This strategy scaffolds students' independent use of morphological analysis. Students write unknown words on the chart, identify prefixes, suffixes, and bases, and use them as clues to the meaning, thereby using morphological analysis as a problem-solving tool. Instruction in morphological analysis supports vocabulary knowledge, particularly when it comes to complex words (Bowers, Kirby, and Deacon 2010; Crosson et al. 2021; Nagy, Carlisle, and Goodwin 2013).

Materials

- *Meaning Morphs* (page 80)
- text selection

Process

1. Distribute *Meaning Morphs* to students, or have them create the chart in their Word Engineer notebooks.

2. Ask students to pay attention to words they do not know as they read a text selection. Students can work independently or in pairs to record the unknown words. Students should examine no more than three words per reading selection.

3. After students have finished reading, demonstrate how to analyze a word for its parts using the *Meaning Morphs* chart.

4. Ask students to look up the meanings of any prefixes, suffixes, or bases they do not know. (Anchor charts providing some of this information are a useful resource.) Encourage students to guess the meaning of the words based on the clues provided by the word parts.

5. Discuss the words as a class, and ask students to explain the definitions they created along with their thinking.

6. Review the actual definitions as a class, comparing and contrasting them to students' guesses.

7. Have students use the strategy throughout the year in different content areas to reinforce and practice morphological awareness.

Differentiation

This strategy can be differentiated based on students' grade level and knowledge of morphology. For example, words chosen from fifth-grade texts will be far more complex than those from third grade and will contain more Greek and Latin derivations. Students with more novice skills may need scaffolding such as prefix/suffix definition charts or a focus on finding words containing base words and bound morphemes.

Meaning Morphs *Example*

Unknown Word	Bases	Prefixes	Suffixes	My Guess Definition
autobiography	bio (life) graph (write)	auto- (self)		To write about your own life
incredible	cred (believe)	in- (not)	-ible (capable of)	To not be able to believe
revival	viv (to live)	re- (again)	-al (process of)	The process of making someone come back to life

Name: _____ Date: _____

Meaning Morphs

Directions: Record unknown words from the text. Look up unknown prefixes, suffixes, or bases. Use the information to write each word's definition.

Unknown Word	Bases	Prefixes	Suffixes	My Guess Definition

Word Spokes

Objectives

- Use combined knowledge of all letter-sound correspondences, syllabication patterns, and morphology to accurately determine the meaning of multisyllabic words.

- Use common, grade-appropriate Greek and Latin affixes and roots as clues to the meaning of a word.

Background Information

Word Spokes (Rasinski et al. 2011) is a terrific strategy for applying students' knowledge of affixes to meaning-making. The Build Words with Prefixes (page 27) and Build Words with Suffixes (page 31) strategies focus on the sound and structure of affixes as tools for decoding; here we add the meaning of affixes to build vocabulary. By using affixes and a variety of base words as clues to determine word meanings, students become familiar with frequently occurring word parts and can use this knowledge to determine the meaning of similar unknown words. Word Spokes can also be used to study base and root words. The base can be placed in the center of the wheel, and students can generate lists of words that share it, using the root or base in addition to their affix knowledge to determine word meanings.

Materials

- *Word Spokes* (page 84)
- list of affixes

Process

1. Identify the affixes students will be learning. You may wish to use affixes from Build Words with Prefixes and/or Build Words with Suffixes lessons. Explain that each affix has a meaning and that knowledge of these meanings helps us figure out the meanings of words using the affix. For example, *pre-* means "before" and *-est* means "most."

2. Model how to generate a list of words containing the same affix, for example, *pretest, preview, predict*. Elicit additional words from students.

3. Guide students in a discussion of the meanings of the words on the list, paying attention to combining the meanings of the affix and the base word. For example, *pretest*: *pre–* means "before," so *pretest* means "to test before something (such as further instruction)."

4. Place students in small groups, and give each group a large piece of chart paper. Have them draw a Word Spokes graphic organizer. Or have students work in pairs on the *Word Spokes* activity sheet (page 84). Assign each group an affix, and have students generate as many words as possible using the affix, writing each word on a spoke with its definition and a small visual if possible.

5. Review the completed Word Spokes organizers and definitions with the whole class.

Differentiation

Students who need additional support may benefit from using a dictionary or other reference tools. You may wish to scaffold this lesson for some students by first focusing on prefixes, since it is easier to look up words by their shared prefix. You may also scaffold this lesson by providing students with a list of words that contain a common affix and reviewing the words with students in advance so they can identify and underline the common affix. Once the affix has been defined, students can complete the Word Spokes organizer using the words.

Word Spokes *Example*

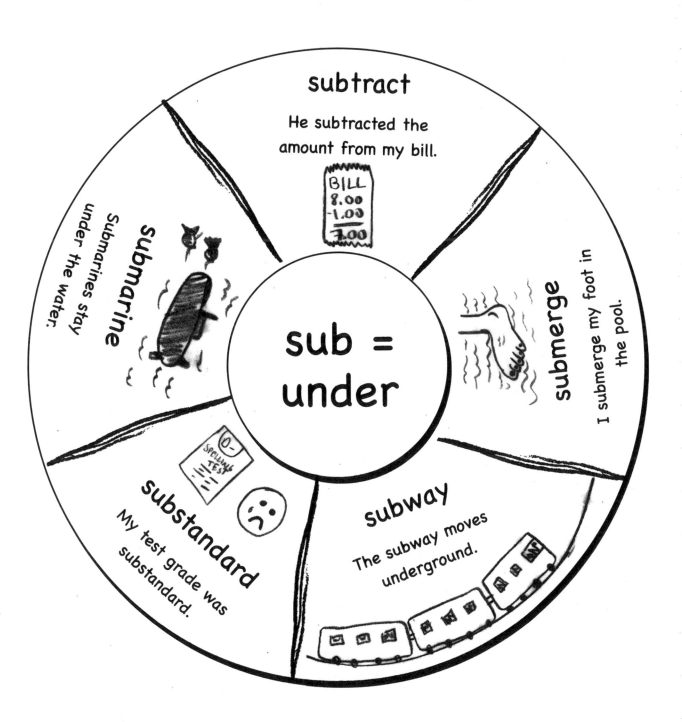

Name: _____ Date: _____

Word Spokes

Directions: Write the affix and its meaning in the small circle. In the large circle, write words that have the same affix. Define the words or write sentences using them. Draw pictures of the meanings.

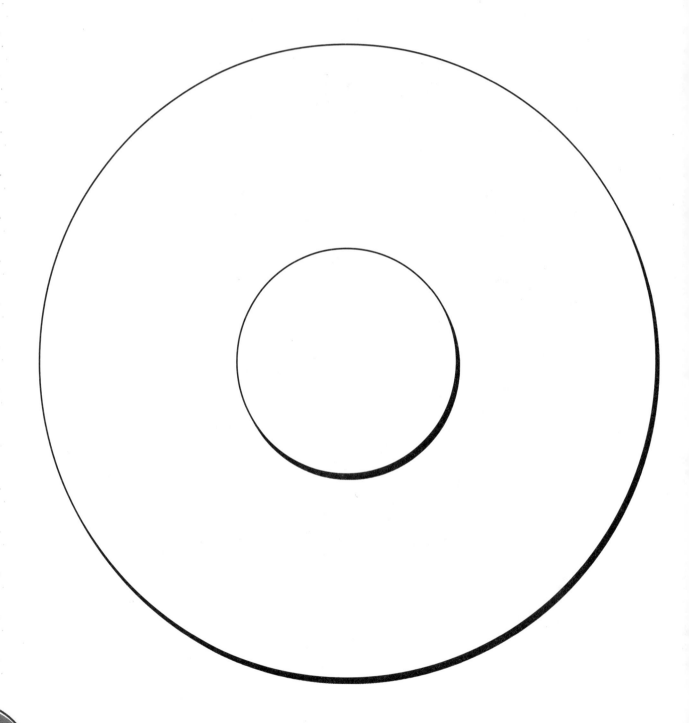

Interactive Word Walls

Objectives

- Describe the relationship between a series of historical events, scientific ideas or concepts, or steps in technical procedures in a text, using language that pertains to time, sequence, and cause/effect.

- Determine the meaning of general academic and domain-specific words and phrases in a grade-relevant topic or subject area.

Background Information

Interactive Word Walls support the development of word knowledge and content knowledge. Research has found that word walls become instructional tools when they are based on a theme, are organized conceptually, include student-created materials and visual cues, and are used during discussion and writing (Jackson, Huerta, and Garza 2020). As students read and discuss thematically related texts and encounter new learning, they are encouraged to add to the Interactive Word Wall. This creates a sense of ownership of the wall and, in turn, of their learning. Demonstrating conceptual connections and being repeatedly exposed to concept-related words strengthens the lexical and semantic networks students can draw from when learning new information and helps them imprint the words and associations into long-term memory (Cabell and Hwang 2020).

Materials

- bulletin board or chart paper
- index cards

Process

1. Prior to beginning a unit of study or reading sets of connected text, select important target vocabulary. For example, if students are studying the different forms of water, words such as *solid*, *liquid*, *vapor*, *steam*, *frozen*, and *moist* would be appropriate.

2. Consider how to structure the word wall so the words are accessible for students: Can the words be organized in a hierarchy, by similarities and differences in meanings, by shades of meanings? Is the concept being studied cyclical or sequential?

3. Write the target vocabulary words on index cards. Choose a prominent place in the classroom to be the home of the word wall. Post the index cards there.

4. Have students draw or find pictures that represent examples of the words and place the examples near the words. As students build knowledge of the words and related concepts, the class may decide to group or regroup the words into different categories to demonstrate connections between words and the concepts they represent. This reflects the interactive nature of the word wall. Rather than being solely about the words, it serves as a visual representation of conceptual knowledge. For content-area learning, items such as data, graphs, charts, primary source documents, and mathematical representations can be added.

5. Refer to the Interactive Word Wall frequently so it becomes a reference tool for students. Be sure to add to it throughout the period of learning related to the topic. Find ways to use it during instruction. Students can reference the wall when writing and spelling, before and after reading, and while answering questions. Encourage students to use the words in their speaking and writing by having discussions in class about and with the word wall.

Differentiation

Interactive Word Walls can be differentiated in endless ways to represent concepts and word learning across all content areas. Words can be supported with or even replaced with visual images for students who may benefit from this support. Students can be encouraged to copy the word wall into their notebooks and individualize their learning by adding to it during independent reading and inquiry. Sentence stems can be made available to support students in using the knowledge represented on the word wall when speaking and writing.

Bricks and Mortar

Objectives

- Determine the meaning of general academic and domain-specific words or phrases in a grade-level text.
- Use precise language and domain-specific vocabulary to explain the topic.

Background Information

Adapted from Zwiers's (2022) and Dutro and Moran's (2003) work with academic language with English learners, the Bricks and Mortar strategy benefits all students by developing the use of content vocabulary and general academic language in speaking and writing. Speaking and writing about concepts and ideas, particularly in content-area learning, requires knowledge of content-specific terminology (referred to as "brick" words) and academic language that expresses transitions, sequencing, connections, and other abstract language ("mortar" words). Practice in building sentences with bricks and mortar words reinforces language structure and syntax and builds academic understanding of the topic.

Materials

- *Bricks and Mortar* (page 89)

Process

1. List five to seven key (brick) content-specific vocabulary words from the current topic of study on the board. Review and discuss the definitions.

2. Direct students to record the brick words on the *Bricks and Mortar* activity sheet. For an additional challenge, they can organize the words on their sheets in ways that demonstrate knowledge of process, sequence, hierarchy, and so on as applicable.

3. Provide a reference list of mortar words relevant to the topic that can be used to express conceptual knowledge, and ask students to create sentences that combine as many brick and mortar words together as they can. Explain that these sentences should describe what they have learned about the topic in the current unit of study. Students can use the *Bricks and Mortar* activity sheet to record their responses. Encourage students to share their responses orally as well.

Differentiation

Provide students who need extra support with images that help represent the brick words and with sentence frames using the mortar words. Students who are ready for more challenge can be encouraged to revise their sentences by combining them by adding mortar words.

Bricks and Mortar *Example*

Brick Words

American Revolution   Britain   colonists

independence   Patriots   Loyalists

Boston Tea Party

Mortar Words

divided   resulted in   as a result of

between   caused   perspectives

supported

Using brick and mortar words to write sentences

The colonists were angry about Britain putting a tax on tea and that resulted in the Boston Tea Party. The colonists went on the ships and threw all of the tea into the harbor to protest. As a result of the Boston Tea Party, the American Revolution started.

The American Revolution divided some friends, families, and neighbors. People had different perspectives on the war for independence. Colonists who supported Britain were called Loyalists, and colonists who supported independence were called Patriots.

Name: _____ Date: _____

Bricks and Mortar

Directions: Write the brick words and the mortar words. Write sentences using the words to explain what you learned. Draw boxes around the brick words. Underline the mortar words.

Brick Words

Mortar Words

Using brick and mortar words to write sentences

Genre Study

Objectives

- Identify the characteristics of different genres.
- Read and comprehend literary and informational texts.

Background Information

Identifying and understanding the features of a variety of genres enables comprehension by equipping readers with a sense of how ideas are organized in a text (Dewitz et al. 2020). Knowledge of text organization can help a reader set a purpose for reading, anticipate events, make inferences about characters, and find important facts, details, and ideas. Reading across genres and doing deep study of specific genres can be motivational as students begin to identify and develop reading preferences. Reading across genres also supports writing, as students become familiar with styles, themes, and elements of a genre that can be applied to their own writing. Best practices for teaching genre include immersing students by reading several selections in each genre and providing instruction on their elements and features.

Materials

- mentor texts that exemplify a specific genre
- *The Genre Collector* (page 93)

Process

1. Select mentor texts that exemplify a specific genre. Read, or have students read, the mentor texts. Depending on the text, you may provide students with copies, have groups of students share copies, or read aloud to the whole class from a single text.

2. Model, using think-aloud, how you identify the features of the genre in the mentor text. List these on an anchor chart for students' future reference during the unit and to support them during independent reading. This anchor chart can also reinforce vocabulary important to understanding the elements of the genre.

3. Ask students to share what they know about the features, and give them time to explore a sample text of the genre. Have them share examples they found during their reading or listening. Encourage a thorough discussion of the mentor text by prompting students to think deeply about the purposes, features, and elements of genre.

4. Provide each student with a copy of *The Genre Collector* activity sheet. As students continue to explore the mentor text or another text, give them time to identify, explain, and record the elements of the genre found in the text. Have students share their findings with partners or in small groups.

5. Allow students time to reflect on their preferences for the genre.

6. Once students are familiar with *The Genre Collector* activity sheet, they can use it independently to record information about other assigned texts or independent reading selections.

Differentiation

Providing students with a reference for the elements and features of specific genres is a helpful scaffold. The features of a genre can be listed on anchor charts, bookmarks, or cards, and students can add the list to a reading notebook. This will support students as they complete *The Genre Collector* activity sheets, giving them clues and vocabulary support as they explain what they have found in the text.

The Genre Collector *Example*

Title: Around the World in 80 Days

Author: Jules Verne (adapted by Dona Herweck Rice)

Genre: Adventure Fiction

Write about elements in the text. Include details that let you know the genre.

Adventure fiction usually has to have a journey or a quest to do something. In Around the World in 80 Days, they are trying to complete their trip in this short amount of time to win a bet. That is like a journey and a quest. Also, there is usually more than one protagonist, and sometimes Fogg is the protagonist and sometimes Passepartout is. And they are kind of like heroes in the story. In adventure novels the good characters, the protagonists aren't always all good, they have flaws and Fogg and Passepartout are not perfect at all. Adventure books also move fast in their plot and there is a lot of action. There is a lot of action in this story because they go to a lot of places and are in a race to win.

Did you enjoy this text? Do you enjoy this genre? Explain why or why not.

I did like this story. I liked to read about the places they went to and the crazy things that happened to them, and at the end there had been a detective following them the whole time and they didn't even know! I like reading adventure books because they are exciting and they usually take place in cool places.

Name: _____ Date: _____

The Genre Collector

Directions: Read the assigned text or book. Write about it.

Title: _____

Author: _____

Genre: _____

Write about elements in the text. Include details that let you know the genre.

_____

_____

_____

_____

_____

_____

_____

Did you enjoy this text? Do you enjoy this genre? Explain why or why not.

_____

_____

_____

_____

_____

_____

Sentence Anagrams

Objectives

- Use knowledge of language and its conventions when writing, speaking, reading, or listening.
- Choose words and phrases to convey ideas precisely.

Background Information

Sentence Anagrams is a strategy for developing syntactic awareness. Knowledge of how words and phrases can be combined to make meaning becomes ever more critical as students in the upper elementary grades encounter increasingly complex text. Research shows that syntactic awareness contributes to effective word reading and reading comprehension. Anagrams are a form of wordplay in which the letters of a word can be rearranged to form new words. With Sentence Anagrams, teachers select a well-crafted sentence, break it apart into smaller phrases, then have students put it back together and compare their results with the original.

Materials

- sentences from texts familiar to students
- Sentence Anagram activity sheet (created by teacher)

Process

1. Prepare by selecting a well-crafted sentence from a text students are familiar with or will be reading. Or, use or create a sentence that includes words encountered in recent word study lessons. Chunk the sentence into short phrases. Phrases should follow appropriate conventions and contain meaning; do not break up the sentence randomly.

2. Display the phrases out of order. Alternately, give students the phrases on small strips of paper to manipulate physically.

3. Explain that the phrases need to be rearranged to make a complete sentence that follows correct English grammar. Students may rearrange or add conjunctions or punctuation as needed to make their sentences grammatically correct.

4. Model the technique, thinking aloud to explain grammatical features you want students to notice (prepositional phrases, appositives, coordinating conjunctions, etc.). Elicit input from students as you model the technique.

5. Create a Sentence Anagram activity sheet with practice sentences chunked into phrases that are out of order. Distribute the sheet to students, and have them work in pairs or independently to combine the phrases into complete sentences.

6. Discuss students' work, inviting students to share their sentences and explain their thinking. Be sure to share the original sentence and compare students' results to the original sentence.

Differentiation

Some students may benefit from starting with sentence anagrams at the word level. Begin by mixing up the words in simpler sentences and having students rearrange them to form complete sentences. Gradually expand the number of words and the complexity of the sentence structure to include limited or simple phrases. You may wish to provide additional scaffolding by capitalizing the first word of the sentence and including punctuation after the last word as clues for students.

Example

The following example is from *Island of the Blue Dolphins* (O'Dell 1960).

Original Sentence: "Everyone in our tribe had two names, the real one which was secret and was seldom used, and one which was common, for if people use your secret name it becomes worn out and loses its magic."

Phrases

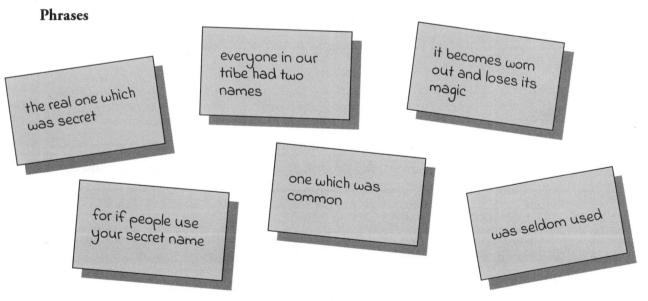

the real one which was secret

everyone in our tribe had two names

it becomes worn out and loses its magic

for if people use your secret name

one which was common

was seldom used

New Sentence: Everyone in our tribe had two names, one which was common and the real one which was secret was seldom used for if people use your secret name it becomes worn out and loses its magic.

Signal Sleuths

Objectives

- Acquire and use grade-appropriate general academic and domain-specific words and phrases, including those that signal precise actions, emotions, or states of being and that are basic to a particular topic.

Background Information

Signal Sleuths is a strategy to enhance comprehension by identifying words that signal text structure. These "signal," or connecting, words show relationships between ideas and concepts, link ideas together, and indicate transitions from one idea to another. Knowledge of these words has a positive effect on reading comprehension because the words provide clues about how ideas are connected (August et al. 2020). Learning to recognize signal words and identify text structure helps readers monitor comprehension, make inferences and predictions, and focus on key concepts. Recognizing signal words also builds students' word consciousness by focusing attention on how and when words are used, along with their meanings. Students may need explicit instruction on signal words for each text structure prior to identifying them independently. Once students are familiar with signal words, they can independently hunt for and record the words while reading.

Materials

- *Signal Sleuths* (page 99)
- text selection

Process

1. Select a section of text and identify its primary text structure. Be sure to select text that contains an easily identifiable pattern. Prepare a grade-level-appropriate list of the signal words associated with this text structure.

2. Provide students with copies of *Signal Sleuths*, or give them sticky notes they can use to make notes. Explain that authors use signal words to provide readers with specific clues about how a text will be organized and what information is most important.

3. Model how to identify signal words in the text, and then demonstrate how to annotate the text to highlight important ideas and information gleaned from the text pattern.

4. Ask students to read a section independently and make note of signal words in the section. When students are finished, ask them to share the signal words with partners.

5. Discuss how identifying signal words helps us understand what we are reading. Point out that learning signal words also helps us use different text structures when we are writing.

Differentiation

Students who need extra support will benefit from having a list of signal words for the specific text structure available as a reference while they read. Additionally, some students may benefit from breaking the reading into smaller sections and using a highlighter to mark the signal words. This activity can be extended by having students identify an appropriate graphic organizer for the text structure they identified.

Examples of Common Signal Words

Text Structure	Signal Words	Graphic Organizer
cause-effect	as a result, as a consequence, because, brought about, consequently, due to, for, in order to, led to, since, so, that is why, the effect of, the outcome was, the reason was, therefore	
compare-contrast	also, although, as opposed to, as well as, both, different, however, like, much as, not only...but also, on the contrary, on the other hand, same, similar(ly), too, yet	
description	all, for example, for instance, in addition, in fact, most(ly), some, specifically, such as, to illustrate, too	
problem-solution	answer, challenge, conclusion, dilemma, fortunately, issue, led to, one challenge, problem, question, solved, therefore, trouble, unfortunately	
sequence of events	after, before, during, eventually, finally, first, following, immediately, in the end, last(ly), meanwhile, next, now, then, when, while	

Signal Sleuths Example

Text Structure: Compare and Contrast

Page or Paragraph	Signal Words	What These Words Tell Me
1	But in science	This was contrasting the two meanings of the word power.
7	They both	The new solar generator and the older solar generator both use the sun for power.
8	Unlike older models	The new solar generator does not need full sun to make power the way the older ones did.

Signal Sleuths

Directions: As you read, look for signal words that connect ideas and give clues about the structure of the text. Explain how the signal words are used in the text.

Text Structure:_____

Page or Paragraph	Signal Words	What These Words Tell Me

Magnet Words

Objectives

- Determine the main idea of a text and explain how it is supported by key words and details; summarize the text.

Background Information

Magnet Words (Buehl 2014) is a comprehension strategy that helps students explain their understanding of important concepts as they read complex text. This strategy supports comprehension while developing students' syntactic awareness. *Syntactic awareness* refers to the ability to monitor the relationships among the words in a sentence in order to understand while reading or composing (Sedita 2019). When reading, students focus on key words and consider how the words might work together to create meaning, asking themselves which words are the "magnets"—the words that "attract" the main ideas and capture the meaning of the passage. This strategy supports building content knowledge through reading informational text and helps students process their understanding of what they read through writing a summary.

Materials

- *Magnet Words and Summary* (page 103)
- text selection

Process

1. Explain the idea of *magnet words*. Just as magnets attract metal, magnet words are words that "attract" important information. These words can be found in titles, headings, or bold or highlighted words in a text.

2. Model by reading aloud a short passage in the text. Students can read along silently. Think aloud as you process key concepts and ideas in the passage by identifying one or two magnet words that capture the main idea. Begin a word map on the board or on chart paper, and write one of the magnet words in the center.

3. Using the model magnet word, discuss as a class additional words, phrases, or details that are attracted to the magnet word (words that support the main idea). Record these additional words, phrases, or details on the word map, and connect them to the magnet word.

4. Generate a concise summary using the magnet words and the additional words, phrases, or details. Discuss the need to add connective language so the summary makes sense and expresses the main idea in a way that is grammatically correct.

5. Provide students with copies of *Magnet Words and Summary*, and have them read a new passage independently or in pairs. As they read, they should select magnet words and details to record on the activity sheet. They can work with partners or independently to write summaries for their magnet words.

6. Allow students time to share their summaries with the class.

Differentiation

Model this strategy multiple times, and provide students with opportunities to engage in the process as a class. You may wish to have students work in cooperative groups to support one another in identifying the magnet words and writing the summaries. Alternately, scaffold the lesson for students as needed by providing an activity sheet partially completed. The magnet word or details could be completed, or the activity sheet could include a paragraph frame for the summary.

Magnet Words and Summary *Example*

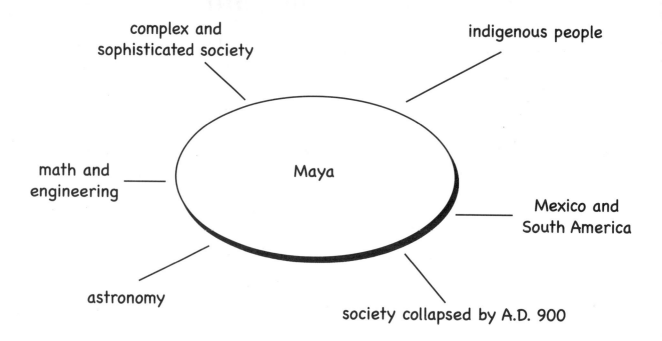

Summary:

The Maya were an indigenous people from Mexico and South America. They created a complex and sophisticated society. They are known for accomplishing great things in math, engineering, and astronomy. The civilization collapsed by the year A.D. 900.

Magnet Words and Summary

Directions: In the oval, write the topic of the text. This is a magnet word. Write details about the magnet word around the oval. Draw lines connecting the details to the magnet word. Use the magnet word and the details to write a summary.

Summary: _____

_____

_____

_____

_____

_____

Concept Mapping

Objective

- Describe the relationship between events, ideas, or concepts in a grade-level text on a specific topic.

Background Information

Concept Mapping is an effective strategy for visually organizing information related to concepts discussed in informational texts (Hattie 2009; Horton et al. 1993). Before reading, a Concept Map is created with students, eliciting their prior knowledge. The teacher adds to the map to build students' conceptual knowledge. Teachers and students continue to add to the map during reading, after engaging with multimedia such as viewing a video, or after examining images related to the topic. The purpose of the strategy is less about the creation of a product and more about developing a process students can use to map and illustrate their own understanding of relationships and connections between concepts.

Materials

- text selection

Process

1. Review the material students will be reading. Identify the important concepts in the reading, and note the ideas, words, and phrases that are related to these concepts.

2. Explain the purpose of a concept map to students, and discuss how it can be effectively used as a learning tool. Present the topic of the concept map, and discuss its relationship to the text students will be reading. Ask students to share their prior knowledge and ideas related to the topic. Create a concept map using their ideas. Clarify any misinformation and add concepts you identified during step 1. Identify the relationships and connections between those concepts.

3. Have students copy the concept map into their notebooks. Alternately, you may wish to skip this step and post a class copy of the concept map on chart paper.

4. Have students read the selection, using the concept map as a study guide. If students have their own copies, they can highlight pertinent information and take notes on the maps. If using a whole-class concept map, regroup after reading to record additional learning on the map.

Differentiation

It may be useful to preview some of the information with students who need extra support. Discuss specific concepts and connections with these students before engaging in the whole-class discussion. You may want to place students in pairs so that they can work cooperatively to complete their maps. It may also be helpful for some students to color code the relationships represented on the map. Encourage students who have extensive prior knowledge of the topic to expand their maps by making connections to related knowledge.

Concept Map Example

```
┌─────────────────┐        ┌──────────────────┐
│   forms cloud   │────────│ clouds anvil-shaped │
└─────────────────┘        └──────────────────┘
        │
┌──────────────────────────┐
│ humid air pushed high in │
│       atmosphere         │
│  cools down as it goes up│
└──────────────────────────┘
        │
  ┌──────────┐
  │   rain   │
  └──────────┘
        │
┌──────────────┐   ╭─────────────────────╮   ┌──────────┐
│ strong storm │───│  Thunderstorms are  │───│ lightning │
└──────────────┘   │     dangerous.      │   └──────────┘
                   ╰─────────────────────╯         │
        │                                ┌────────────────────┐
   ┌──────────┐                          │ electrical charges │
   │  thunder │                          │   build in clouds  │
   └──────────┘                          └────────────────────┘
        │                                          │
┌────────────────────────┐               ┌──────────────────┐
│ temperature of air along│               │ charges increase │
│ lightning bolt is super │               │  and turn into   │
│          hot            │               │  electricity as  │
└────────────────────────┘               │    lightning     │
        │                                 └──────────────────┘
┌────────────────────┐                            │
│ heat makes air expand│                  ┌──────────────────┐
│     extra fast      │                  │ travels in cloud or│
└────────────────────┘                  │    hits Earth     │
        │                                 └──────────────────┘
┌────────────────────────┐
│ creates shock waves that│
│  make sound of thunder  │
└────────────────────────┘
```

Facts-Questions-Responses (FQR)

Objectives

- Ask and answer questions to demonstrate understanding of a text, referring explicitly to the text as the basis for the answers.

- Determine the main idea of a text; recount the key details and explain how they support the main idea.

Background Information

As students engage with ever-more-complex informational text, they need to be able to organize and make sense of names, dates, processes, procedures, and other statements of fact to build their content knowledge. Facts-Questions-Responses (Harvey and Goudvis 2017) is a note-taking and reading comprehension strategy to help students understand and remember facts and information they read. As students read independently, they note key ideas, generate questions, and respond to their facts, questions, or both. This strategy may need intensive modeling at first, before gradually releasing responsibility to students. It is best taught as a whole- or small-group teacher-directed lesson several times. Students should work toward using this strategy independently while they read and then use their notes as the basis of class discussion.

Materials

- text selection
- *Facts-Questions-Responses* (page 109)

Process

1. Introduce the text selection, and review the *Facts-Questions-Responses* activity sheet with students.

2. Model reading the first paragraph and using *Facts-Questions-Responses* to take notes. The process is as follows:

   a. Students take notes on key ideas they consider to be facts.

   b. Students generate questions they have about the facts. The questions often reflect students making connections, attempting to clarify misunderstandings or fill gaps in their knowledge, or setting a purpose for future learning about the topic.

   c. They then respond to their facts, questions, or both. Here, students provide personal reactions to the text as they explain their thinking and understanding and make inferences and connections.

3 Conduct a think-aloud to model your thought processes, beginning with facts and questions. Then, model adding responses if applicable.

4. Direct students to read the selection, or a segment of the selection, and record facts from the selection and questions they may have.

5. Conduct a class discussion of the facts students gleaned and the questions students generated.

6. Model thoughtful responses to the facts and questions through a think-aloud and a whole-class discussion.

7. Continue this process to read the remainder of the text selection.

8. As students become more familiar with FQR, gradually release responsibility by having students shift from working as a whole class, to working in small groups or with partners, to independent reading and note-taking. Conclude with whole-class discussions.

Differentiation

Some students may benefit from using sticky notes to annotate or code the text before recording their notes on their activity sheets. After they read, they can engage in a discussion with the teacher or partners to be sure they have accurately labeled information as facts before recording it. Additionally, providing question stems or sentence starters as scaffolds for the Questions and Responses columns may be helpful for some students. FQR can also be used as a listening comprehension activity or while viewing video resources.

Sentence Stems		
Facts	**Questions**	**Responses**
I read . . .	I wonder . . .	I think . . .
I noticed . . .	Who?	I understand . . .
The text said . . .	What?	I question . . .
I learned . . .	Where?	I feel . . .
I remember . . .	When?	I believe . . .
	Why?	
	How?	

Facts-Questions-Responses *Example*

Title: Saving Migratory Birds

Facts	Questions	Responses
Scientists use technology to track migration. Migration means animals (or birds) move to different places when the weather changes. Some migrate far but some just move to a different spot in the same place. Migration can be hard and dangerous for the birds. It can be hard to help migrating birds in danger because they live in different places at different times.	I wonder if you feed birds during the winter if they would stay or would they still migrate? Which places have the most migrating birds? What kind of birds don't migrate?	I believe that technology is a good way to help save the birds that might be extinct soon, like tracking the baby birds. I learned all places in the world have many migrating birds. They follow paths called flyways. I read that in places where the weather stays warm, most birds don't have to migrate, like pelicans.

Name: _____ Date: _____

Facts-Questions-Responses

Directions: Record interesting facts you learn. Write questions you have. Write your responses to what you read or to your questions.

Title: _____

Facts	Questions	Responses

Rank-Ordering Retell (ROR)

Objective

- Determine two or more main ideas of a text and explain how they are supported by key details; summarize the text.

Background Information

Rank-Ordering Retell (ROR) (Hoyt 2002) helps students learn to identify the main idea and key supporting details of a text. To effectively summarize what they have read, students need to learn how to determine the most important ideas, the moderately important ideas, and the less important ideas. With ROR, students write phrases they consider important to the topic and then categorize the phrases as the most important, moderately important, or least important concepts in the text. Key details, central messages, and important lessons from the text are classified as most important, while less important details and nonessential information are placed in the moderately important or least important categories. This strategy can be used with narrative and expository text across the content areas.

Materials

- *Rank-Ordering Retell* (page 113)
- text selection
- strips of paper

Process

1. Distribute several strips of paper to each student. Explain that as they read the selection, they should write phrases they consider important to the topic on the strips. The phrases can be taken directly from the text or inferred by students and should describe the information in the reading.

2. Give students the *Rank-Ordering Retell* activity sheet and have them use it to evaluate and sort their strips into three categories: most important, moderately important, and least important.

3. Instruct students to work with the most important and least important first, as these are the easiest to evaluate. Have students justify their decisions to sort the phrases into the different categories.

4. Pair students, and have them compare the phrases they wrote on the strips and explain to their partners how they ranked them.

5. Conduct a group discussion about the information students chose and their rankings. Ask students to identify which ideas would be the most helpful if they had to write a summary.

Differentiation

Some students may need extra support, particularly if the topic of the text is unfamiliar or linguistically complex. Scaffold the task by completing some of the strips for students. ROR can be extended by having students write a short summary of the reading based on how they categorized the phrases.

Rank-Ordering Retell (ROR) *Example*

Narrative Example

Text: <u>Horrible Harry and the Ant Invasion</u> by Suzy Kline

Most important ideas:

Harry loves ants and is disappointed when he loses his job as the classroom ant monitor.

Moderately important ideas:

Harry thinks of an activity with ant words to impress his teacher and win his job back.

Least important ideas:

Mrs. Foxworth, the secretary, is afraid of ants.

Expository Example

Text: <u>The National Road</u>

Most important ideas:

The National Road helped people move west.

Moderately important ideas:

Many people helped to build it over many years.

Least important ideas:

Old roads were made of stone or planks of wood.

Name: _____ Date: _____

Rank-Ordering Retell (ROR)

Directions: On strips of paper, write important phrases from the text. Then, sort the strips into the groups shown below.

Text: _____

Most important ideas:

Moderately important ideas:

Least important ideas:

One-Sentence Paraphrase

Objective

- Determine the main idea of a text; summarize the text.

Background Information

One-Sentence Paraphrase is a strategy that encourages students to demonstrate their understanding of what they have read in one concise statement. Like summarizing, paraphrasing helps students translate the ideas in a text into their own words. This skill is critical as students encounter increasingly complex text and need to be able to condense large amounts of information into the main points. One-Sentence Paraphrase places the emphasis on learning the main points rather than remembering all of the specific details. Practicing this strategy helps students discern the most important ideas in a text and ignore non-essential ones. Articulating a concise understanding of material also supports the development of content knowledge.

Materials

- *One-Sentence Paraphrase* (page 117)
- text selection

Process

1. Prepare by previewing a text selection to determine appropriate stopping points for each one-sentence paraphrase. This is typically after each paragraph, although you may wish to break apart complex paragraphs that contain many details.

2. Provide each student with a *One-Sentence Paraphrase* activity sheet. Explain that the class will be reading the selection together and stopping at points to write a one-sentence paraphrase. Share that *paraphrase* means to explain the main idea in your own words.

3. Read the first paragraph or section together.

4. Direct students to cover the paragraph with their activity sheet or another piece of paper and write one sentence that reflects their understanding of what they just read.

5. Have students share their sentences. Ask students to compare their sentences to their classmates' sentences, looking for similarities and differences.

6. Continue the process until the entire selection has been read.

Differentiation

This strategy can be used in a variety of ways. Students can engage in the activity as a warm-up to summarize prior knowledge or as a summary activity at the end of a lesson. Scaffold the process by providing key words for students to look for in the text or by directing students to focus on a specific who, what, when, where, or why.

One-Sentence Paraphrase *Example*

Title of Text: Hand to Paw: Protecting Animals

One-Sentence Paraphrase #1

Many different kinds of animals hunt, mate, and build homes all over the earth.

One-Sentence Paraphrase #2

People have admired and depended on wild animals for thousands of years.

One-Sentence Paraphrase #3

A domesticated animal lives with people on a farm or in their home.

One-Sentence Paraphrase #4

Humans are animals too, but we are different because we think and make choices.

One-Sentence Paraphrase

Directions: *Paraphrase* means "restate using your own words." Read each section of the text. Write one sentence about it using your own words. Your sentence should tell the main idea.

Title of Text: _____

One-Sentence Paraphrase #1 _____

_____

_____

One-Sentence Paraphrase #2 _____

_____

_____

One-Sentence Paraphrase #3 _____

_____

_____

One-Sentence Paraphrase #4 _____

_____

_____

One-Sentence Paraphrase #5 _____

_____

_____

Question Journal

Objectives

- Refer to details and examples in a text when explaining what the text says explicitly and when drawing inferences from the text.

- Determine the main idea of a text and explain how it is supported by key details; summarize the text.

- Ask and answer questions to demonstrate understanding of a text, referring explicitly to the text as the basis for the answers.

Background Information

Question Journals are an informal but effective way to help students identify key details in an informational text. Students keep Question Journals throughout the year and use them to answer questions they are asked and to generate questions of their own. This strategy gradually releases the responsibility of monitoring comprehension through questioning from teachers to students, moving students toward independence. Students generate questions before, during, and after reading, which reinforces skills such as setting a purpose, monitoring and clarifying, and being an active reader. Note that students are likely to rely on asking "Right There" and "Think and Search" questions since those are explicit and easy to generate; therefore you may want to provide extensive modeling of "Author and Me" questions.

Materials

- *Question Journal* (page 121)
- text selection
- sticky notes

Process

1. Segment the text into several sections students will read silently. Post the section start and stop points for student reference, or have students mark the sections in the text if appropriate. Have students use sticky notes to mark the end of a section and to record their questions in their notebooks or on the *Question Journal* activity sheet.

2. Share the topic of the reading with students, and allow them a few minutes to preview and skim the text. Tell students to think of questions they may have about the text based on their prior knowledge and the quick scan of the text. Allow time for students to generate questions on their own or in pairs. Have students share some of their questions. Lead a discussion to identify the type of question (see the next page). Have each student generate and record a possible answer to their question.

3. Give students time to read. Then have them answer their questions, citing evidence from the text. If needed, model how to give complete responses to a question, providing detail and text evidence. Explain that "I don't know" is not an acceptable response to a question. If a poor or unanswerable question is asked, model how to think about the question and rephrase, or query the question-asker for explanation and clarification.

4. Prepare students to read the next segment of text. Provide a question for them to consider while they read this section, and encourage them to generate questions of their own. Use this as an opportunity to model asking "Author and Me" questions if appropriate.

5. Assess student readiness to work on the remainder of the text in partners or small groups. The whole class or specific students may need more teacher modeling or support before working independently. Encourage students who are ready to work independently to monitor the questions they ask and answer by using sticky notes or the *Question Journal* activity sheet.

Differentiation

This is a flexible strategy that can be used for whole-class and small-group instruction. Students who need extra support generating questions from the text may find it useful to use the *Question Journal* activity sheet. This resource encourages students to think of a variety of questions while they read. Challenge students by having them research questions that were unanswered by the text.

Types of Questions	
In the Text	**In My Head**
Right There The answer to the question can be found easily and immediately in the text. The words used to create the question are the same words used in the text. **Think and Search** The answer to the question can be found in the text, but the reader may have to combine two parts of the text to arrive at an answer. The words in the question may not directly lead the reader to the answer in the text. The reader has to make connections to arrive at an answer.	**Author and Me** The answer to the question is not found directly in the text. The reader has to think about the information that the author provided, prior knowledge about the topic, and personal experience. The reader has to make connections to answer the question.

Question Journal *Example*

Questions and Answers

Before Reading Questions	Possible Answers	Answers/Evidence
What is Taino? (Right There)	It might be a place Columbus found.	Taino are the native people of the Caribbean. (p. 4)
Did the three ships stay together? (Right There)	I can't imagine they did.	All 3 ships made it to the islands, but one finally had to be abandoned. (p. 7)
What made the journey difficult? (Right There)	I think it would be hard and probably scary and a long trip.	There was almost a mutiny, and the food was rotten. (p. 6)
Why did Columbus want to find a way to Asia? (Right There)	He wanted to find a shorter way there.	He wanted to find a trade route to Asia that was shorter. (p. 4)
During Reading Questions	**Possible Answers**	**Answers/Evidence**
Why did Ferdinand and Isabella fund the expedition? (Think and Search)	They probably wanted to get rich and to get fancy things like gold and spices and jewels from Asia.	They wanted to have an advantage over Portugal in trading to make Spain richer. (p. 5)
Why did Columbus think he landed on the coast of Asia? (Think and Search or Right There)	Maybe he had never been to Asia and didn't know what it looked like?	He didn't know there was land between Europe and Asia, he thought Asia was across from Europe. (p. 8)
After Reading Questions	**Possible Answers**	**Answers/Evidence**
How did Columbus change the lives of the Taino? (Author and Me) What did Ferdinand and Isabella get from the expedition? (Think and Search)	He probably made them slaves and maybe they died from diseases like I learned in 4th grade about the Indigenous Americans.	The Taino were made slaves and many of them died, he ruined their culture. (p. 9)

Name: _____ Date: _____

Question Journal

Directions: Record your questions before and during reading. Label the type of each question. As you read and discuss, write the answers and new questions. After reading, write questions you still have.

Types of Questions

Right There	Think and Search	Author and Me

Questions and Answers

Before Reading Questions	Possible Answers	Answers/Evidence
During Reading Questions	Possible Answers	Answers/Evidence
After Reading Questions	Possible Answers	Answers/Evidence

Annotate and Compare

Objectives

- Read closely to determine what the text says and to make logical inferences from it.
- Cite text evidence to support conclusions drawn from the text.

Background Information

Annotate and Compare is a strategy for teaching readers the valuable skill of annotation. Annotation develops a sophisticated skill set: students practice thinking about important information and main ideas, monitor their understanding, summarize and synthesize in real time as they are reading, and later discuss with peers (Fisher and Frey 2014). Students annotate by "coding" text using markings or symbols to represent new information, points of confusion, connection, and so on. Students highlight unknown words, important facts, and questions they have. For narrative text, students can find and annotate evidence of character traits or the theme, problem, or solution. In informational text, annotations can be made to track main ideas and key details or to make connections between visuals and diagrams and the body of the text.

Materials

- *Annotate and Compare* (page 124)
- text selection
- sticky notes

Process

1. Prepare by selecting a piece of text for students to annotate. The text should provide multiple opportunities for students to practice the various annotation symbols.

2. Explain that annotation involves making notes directly on a text, in the margins or by underlining or highlighting key information. Sticky notes can be used to annotate a nonconsumable text. Show students the basic annotations (see page 124).

3. Conduct a think-aloud, and model how to read a portion of the text and use annotation symbols to mark your thinking.

4. Provide students with the *Annotate and Compare* activity sheets. Distribute sticky notes if you are using nonconsumable texts. Have students read a portion of the text and annotate it.

5. Give students time to share their annotations with partners. Encourage them to explain their annotations to one another and compare and contrast the similarities and differences in what they annotated. They can note these comparisons on the activity sheet.

6. Have a class discussion asking students to share their annotations and thinking. Clarify misunderstandings or misapplication of annotation if necessary.

Differentiation

Scaffold the lesson by introducing the annotations one at a time and providing a series of lessons focused on each annotation symbol. Some students may benefit from hearing the reading selection read aloud as they follow along and make annotations. Encourage students with advanced skills to personalize and extend their annotation key, adding symbols they think will be useful when reading.

Annotate and Compare

Directions: As you read, use the symbols to monitor your thinking. After reading, work with a partner to compare the symbols you both used.

Annotation	When to Use It
_____ ◯ ? !	<u>Underline</u> important information, main points Circle key words, phrases, or points of confusion Questions you have (be sure to write your question) Something that caught your attention or surprised you

Comparing with My Partner

One annotation my partner and I both made:

_____

_____

_____

One annotation that was different:

_____

_____

_____

One annotation I added to my text after discussing with my partner:

_____

_____

_____

SECTION III

Writing

The strategies in this section correspond with key competencies identified in *What the Science of Reading Says about Writing* (Jump and Wolfe 2023). These research-based instructional strategies will help teachers bridge the gap between the science of literacy instruction and classroom practice.

Strategy	Skills and Understandings Addressed			
	Genre Characteristics	Prewriting and Organization	Revise for Purpose	Grammar, Usage, and Mechanics
Genre Analysis	■			
RAFT		■		
Paragraph Frames		■		
Rehearsal		■		
Sentence Composing				■
Sentence Expansion				■
Revising Groups			■	
Picture This			■	

Writing

The connection between reading and writing is complex and intricate, placing the act of reading as a necessary and crucial counterpart to writing. This reading-writing connection is obvious to most educators, yet reading and writing have traditionally been taught as separate subjects (Dewitz et al. 2020), and commonly reading instruction takes precedence over writing. Teachers can face many obstacles when it comes to teaching writing; writing well and teaching it well take time and focus. In some states, standardized testing emphasizes reading and writing absent an explicit focus on writing in the curriculum. Additional obstacles include students' reading abilities, which can hamper their writing abilities and their motivation for writing. Increasingly, however, educators are embracing a combined approach to reading and writing instruction as they recognize the benefits of doing so (Dewitz et al. 2020; Graham and Heibert 2010). Teachers know that given the complex communication realities of the modern world, the ability to write well across a variety of mediums and genres is critical to academic and career success. They also acknowledge that reading and writing are reciprocal processes. Reading and reading instruction can improve the organization and quality of writing. Writing instruction can improve reading fluency and comprehension.

> Effective writing instruction in the upper elementary grades is critical for continued success in both reading and writing. Learning in one area enhances learning in the other.

These points underscore the importance of writing instruction as part of a comprehensive approach to reading and literacy instruction. The development of writing abilities begins early—the primary grades lay the foundation—but effective writing instruction in the upper elementary grades is critical for continued success in both reading and writing. Learning in one area enhances learning in the other. There is ample evidence to suggest that the processes are inseparable and that we should design our instruction considering these interrelationships. Fitzgerald and Shanahan (2000) described this interrelationship when they proposed that reading and writing are independent yet reciprocal processes that share common knowledge and skills; therefore, what one learns in reading can be applied to writing and vice versa. Knowledge and skills are organized into four categories: *metaknowledge*: establishing a purpose, self-monitoring, self-evaluating; *domain knowledge*: vocabulary, topical/content knowledge; *text attributes*: mechanics, grammar, text structure; and *procedural knowledge*: knowing how to approach the writing task, constructing and generating meaning, analyzing, critiquing (Jouhar and Rupley 2020).

From a pedagogical perspective, a comprehensive review of the research supports the following recommendations (Graham et al. 2012b):

- Provide daily time for writing.
- Teach students the writing process and teach students to write for a variety of purposes.
- Teach students to become fluent in handwriting/typing, spelling, and sentence construction.
- Create an engaged community of writers.

The Role of Purpose, Genre, and Process

Writing is a complex, cognitive, self-directed, goal-driven activity that communicates thoughts and ideas (Graham et al. 2012a). As students progress through the upper elementary grades, writing should become an increasingly independent task. Knowledge and practice of the purpose of writing, the genres of writing, and the writing process facilitate independence and skill. Understanding purpose is key to effective writing, as writers consider what they wish to share, the medium and genre appropriate for the task, and to whom they are writing. Students must have practice in writing for a variety of purposes, learning how to argue and persuade,

> Research demonstrates that explicit instruction in each component of the writing process, both in general and related to specific genres, can help students develop as effective writers.

convey information, respond to literature, share an experience, or tell stories for the purpose of entertaining an audience. Each of these purposes reflects the various genres of writing, and each genre connects reading and writing skills differently, relying on a variety of skills and strategies in both unique and complementary ways.

The writing process allows a writer to take a piece of writing from the beginning, the generation of ideas, to the end, producing a published work. This process includes planning, drafting, sharing, revising/editing, publishing, and reflection/evaluation. Effective writers use these components flexibly as guidelines and guideposts for accomplishing writing tasks. Research demonstrates that explicit instruction in each component of the writing process, both in general and related to specific genres, can help students develop as effective writers (Graham et al. 2012a; Koster et al. 2015). Employing a model of gradual release during writing instruction in grades 3 through 5 is an important part of developing independent writers.

The Writing Process

Writing for meaning and expressing oneself to others is intricate and complex work. Using the writing process helps the writer take a piece of writing from the beginning, or brainstorming, to the end, or the published piece. This process is especially important to follow as students write reports, essays, and other assignments. The process at the emergent writing level is usually conducted as a group, though on occasion it is done individually. Students in higher grades who have more familiarity with the writing process can complete it individually.

There are different points to consider at each step of the writing process.

Prewriting

This is the phase during which all writing begins. At this stage, writers generate ideas, brainstorm topics, web ideas together, or talk and think about ideas. Teachers explain that students may get writing ideas from personal experiences, stories, pictures, television, websites, social media, and a variety of other sources.

This phase sets the foundation for a specific piece of writing. Students need to have a clear understanding of a writing assignment (i.e., the prompt) before they are expected to write or report on it. Before brainstorming or prewriting can begin, students need instruction on the genre or format (research report, journal entry, visual presentation, etc.), audience (the teacher, classmates, their families, the school community, etc.), and purpose (to explain, to persuade, to inform, etc.). These elements impact the types of information to brainstorm.

What does prewriting look like?

- analyzing the prompt
- researching a chosen topic, using print and digital sources
- analyzing the characteristics of the intended genre
- examining sample writing pieces
- discussing the topic with the teacher, a partner, or the class
- brainstorming ideas about the topic
- discussing the assessment tool
- creating a graphic organizer to organize ideas and the structure of the writing

Drafting

At the drafting stage of the writing process, students begin to put their ideas on paper. Students need to keep in mind the genre or format, audience, and purpose. For beginning writers, pictures and drawings are usually part of the composition. Teachers should encourage students to write as much as they can on their own throughout the writing process.

Some students struggle with writing in an orderly manner. Graphic organizers, notes, or outlines from the prewriting stage can help students sequence and organize their writing.

What does drafting look like?

- oral rehearsal of what will be written
- focusing on simply putting ideas on paper
- working fairly quickly
- leaving blank spaces for missing words
- approximating spelling
- using notes or graphic organizers to stay focused

Revising/Editing

This phase of writing consists of two parts: revising looks at the organization and structure of the writing, while editing looks at the mechanics of the writing. Students must understand how to do both. When revising, students analyze their writing for the required traits: sequencing words in a step-by-step process, descriptive language in a fictional story, topic sentences and supporting details in a persuasive piece. They also ask questions of their writing: *Does it make sense? Is anything out of order? Should anything be added or deleted?* When editing, students analyze their writing for correct spelling, grammar, and punctuation.

What do revising and editing look like?

- reading the piece aloud to confirm that it makes sense
- adding missing information
- deleting unnecessary, incorrect, or duplicate information
- proofreading for spelling, capitalization, grammar, and punctuation
- self-analysis by students
- conferences with peers or the teacher

Publishing

Publishing allows students to write for an authentic audience and celebrate their hard work. It occurs after the other steps are completed and the student is ready to produce the final copy, which can be handwritten or typed. The goal is to present the written information attractively so others can enjoy it.

What does publishing look like?

- creating a final copy
- adding illustrations, borders, a cover, and so on
- sharing orally
- publishing in a class book
- posting on a classroom website, a blog, a social media site, or another platform

Ensuring that students understand the purpose for crafting a piece of writing and the elements of the genre, along with consistently providing students time to work through the process of writing, will allow them to hone their craft. As they develop as writers, they will become better at expressing their thoughts and ideas within the different genres.

The Role of Conventions, Organization, and Expression

As discussed previously, when students have a firm command of the foundations of reading (decoding and fluency), they can better attend to comprehension of a text. Similarly with writing, when foundational skills are in place, more time and attention can be spent on the craft of writing (Graham et al. 2012b). Strong foundations in phonological awareness, phonemic awareness, and phonics aid in the development of skillful sentence composition and the orthographic knowledge necessary for good writing. Vocabulary and morphology knowledge can give students freedom and flexibility over word choice and expression that allows them to write more freely as opposed to struggling over the choice and spelling of specific words while composing. When these foundations have been laid, writing instruction can focus on the development and polishing of skilled writing, concentrating on generating increasingly complex and sophisticated sentences and interesting, well-organized writing.

Joan Sedita (2019) identifies five strands that contribute to skilled writing:

- **Critical thinking**—Critical thinking and executive functioning, awareness of the writing process, the use of background knowledge
- **Syntax**—How sentences work
- **Text structure**—Types of texts, paragraph structures, organizational patterns, linking and transition words
- **Writing craft**—Word choice, audience, and literary devices
- **Transcription**—Spelling, handwriting, and keyboarding

Effective instruction that supports organization, expression, and proper use of conventions includes the use of mentor texts, embedded writing tasks, and instruction in writing at the sentence level (Hochman and Wexler 2017; Tompkins 2018).

Encouraging Developing Writers

There are a variety of ways to teach students new ideas and to incorporate writing into the curriculum. Finding opportunities to weave together writing experiences and text is critical. In addition to teaching writer's craft for its own sake, writing can be used to explain and communicate learning and understanding, and as a response to reading. Many of the same practices of good readers are also done by good writers; they set goals, make predictions, make inferences, and read selectively. The more students write, the more skilled they will become in both reading and writing. Here are some characteristics of good writers that can inform instructional considerations for developing strong writers in your classroom:

- Writers write all the time. The more experience one has writing, the better writer one becomes. Learning to write takes practice and more practice!

- Writers read a lot. Reading provides a great model for writers as to what the finished product looks like. Students who read will know how to write better than those who do not.

- Writers are aware of correct spelling. These writers use all the resources available and understand the limitations of spell-check programs.

- Writers appreciate critiques and feedback. These writers have a "thick skin" and ask for input and suggestions from many different sources.

- Writers keep a record of their learning and ideas in journals or learning logs. These records can be used to store good writing ideas, document what is being learned, activate prior knowledge, and question what is being learned (Brozo and Simpson 2003; Fisher and Frey 2020). This can also help students avoid writer's block.

- Writers compose for a variety of purposes. Learning to write in a variety of formats makes for a well-rounded, experienced writer. Writers explore different types of writing formats.

- Writers read and edit other people's writing. Such writers look for opportunities to work with others to improve their writing. Peer-editing groups are an excellent way to get feedback and reinforcement from peers. This feedback is important for the self-image of the writer (Gahn 1989). Editing others' work will also help students recognize writing errors, such as an off-topic response, a weak topic sentence, a lack of supporting detail, weak vocabulary, and errors in spelling or grammar.

- Writers think objectively. They are able to step back and really look at their writing.

- Writers read their work aloud! Many errors or additions are discovered when a student listens to the writing being read aloud.

The strategies that follow are designed to support the development of writers. They support flexible, generic structures, processes, and procedures intended to become a regular part of your writing instruction and writing routines.

Genre Analysis

Objective

- Produce clear and coherent writing in which the development and organization are appropriate to task, purpose, and audience.

Background Information

Genre Analysis engages students in examining a mentor text to understand how that type of text is written. As students develop their writing skills, it is essential that they deepen their understanding of the ways audience, purpose, and content set the goals for and influence forms of writing. Genre Analysis helps students develop an awareness of genre conventions and learn about the organization, goals, and function of language in specific genres. When using a genre approach to writing, introduce one genre at a time using Genre Analysis. Once students are familiar with the characteristics of a specific genre, they can move through the writing process to compose their own texts in that genre. This strategy is adapted from activities in Beverly Derewianka's (2020) excellent resource on genre, *Exploring How Texts Work*.

Materials

- *Genre Analysis* (pages 137–138)
- examples of a specific writing genre

Process

1. Choose a writing genre to analyze. Select a mentor text, or collect several strong examples of the genre in the form of short stories, reports, articles, student writing, and so on. Provide a copy of *Genre Analysis* for each student.

2. Explain to students that we can better understand different genres of writing by thinking about what the author is doing in a particular text. We can examine text and ask ourselves the following questions:

   - How is the text organized? (Is it a book written in chapters? A letter with a greeting and closing? Informational writing with headings and subheadings? A recount of an event? An argument? An explanation?)

   - What do you think this text might be used for?

   - Who is the audience for this text? What makes you think that?

   - What do you think the writer is doing? What does the beginning tell us about the text?

- What kind of language is used? What do you notice about the sentences and words?
  - How long are the sentences?
  - What types of punctuation do you see?
  - Are there quotation marks?
  - Do you see any signal words?
  - Do you see any of the same words used many times?
  - Is it past tense? Present tense?
  - Formal or casual?

3. Place students into groups, and give each group a copy of the text or one text from a collection of genre examples. Allow time for students to work collaboratively to analyze and explore the text, considering the questions on the activity sheet.

4. Bring the students back together to share the results of the analysis. Based on the discussion, create a class anchor chart that outlines the features of the genre.

Differentiation

The activity can be used as a whole-class lesson, guiding students step by step through each question, if students are not yet ready to analyze more independently in small groups. As students become more familiar with the genres, they can be moved toward more independence. Extend the activity for students with more advanced knowledge of genre by having them collect and share examples of a genre and eventually evaluate their own and their peers' writing based on their understanding of the genre.

Genre Analysis *Example*

Genre: Formal Letter

Questions	My Notes
How is the text organized?	There is a greeting that says "Dear Mr. Newport." 4 paragraphs A signature: Sincerely, Benny Rivas
What do you think we might use this text for? What makes you think that?	I think we would use this to ask for something or to tell someone about something that happened because it looks like a letter to someone and that's what you might do in a letter.
Who is the audience for this text? What makes you think that?	We think the principal of a school is the audience because it says "Dear Mr. Newport" and the author is talking about his school.
Read the beginning of the text. What do you think the writer is doing? What does the beginning tell us about the text?	The author Benny is introducing himself to Mr. Newport and asking him to let students wear blue sweatshirts as part of the school uniform. We think this letter is going to try and convince the principal to let the students wear blue sweatshirts.
What kind of language is used? What do you notice about the sentences and words? How long are the sentences?	The sentences are short and they sound very serious like the way a kid would talk to their teacher or the principal.
What types of punctuation do you see? Are there quotation marks?	There are commas and periods.
Do you see any signal words? Do you see any of the same words used many times?	There are signal words like first, next, and finally. Benny uses the words "uniform policy" many times.
Is it past tense? Present tense? Formal or casual?	It is present tense.

Name: _____ Date: _____

Genre Analysis

Directions: Examine the mentor text. Answer the questions to learn more about the genre.

Genre: _____

Questions	My Notes
How is the text organized?	
What do you think we might use this text for? What makes you think that?	
Who is the audience for this text? What makes you think that?	
Read the beginning of the text. What do you think the writer is doing? What does the beginning tell us about the text?	

Name: _____ Date: _____

Genre Analysis *(continued)*

Directions: Examine the mentor text. Answer the questions to learn more about the genre.

Genre: _____

Questions	My Notes
What kind of language is used? What do you notice about the sentences and words? How long are the sentences?	
What types of punctuation do you see? Are there quotation marks?	
Do you see any signal words? Do you see any of the same words used many times?	
Is it past tense? Present tense? Formal or casual?	

RAFT

Objective

- Produce clear and coherent writing in which the development and organization are appropriate to task, purpose, and audience.

Background Information

RAFT stands for Role, Audience, Format, and Topic, the key ingredients of writing assignments (Santa, Havens, and Valdes 1995). RAFT is a strategy to help students understand their roles as writers, the audiences they will write for, and how to communicate their ideas effectively across varied formats and purposes for writing. Developing a sense of a purpose and audience is key in effective communication. RAFT writing supports students in considering topics from multiple perspectives, thinking and writing creatively, and developing understanding of main ideas, coherence, and elaboration. RAFT prompts can be designed in ways that require students to write from perspectives other than their own, strengthening their critical and creative thinking skills. RAFT can be implemented in any content area and used for traditional forms of writing as well as formats such as posters, brochures, and multimedia.

Materials

- *RAFT* (page 142)
- sample writing selection

Process

1. Select a short piece of writing with clear, easily identifiable RAFT components. Tell your students that writers need to consider specific elements before they write. Lead a discussion to identify the following elements in the piece:

   - Role: Who or what is the writer?

   - Audience: To whom is the author writing?

   - Format: What is the format of the writing?

   - Topic and strong verb: What is the writing about? What is the purpose of this communication? (The strong verb indicates purpose and tone.)

2. Display the *RAFT* activity sheet and brainstorm with the class a sample RAFT prompt, recording suggestions and determining a role, audience, format, topic, and strong verb. It may be necessary to model how to write responses to a RAFT prompt.

3. Have students work in small groups or individually, writing in response to the RAFT prompt. As students become familiar with RAFT, have them develop the RAFT prompt on their own and then write to the prompt. Alternatively, you can provide part or all of a RAFT prompt for practice, scaffolding student choice until students are ready to work independently.

Differentiation

Introduce each component of RAFT separately to allow students to develop command over each one before moving to the next. As students become more familiar with the strategy, provide multiple choices for one of the components to demonstrate how varying the elements can change the writing. For example, the prompt could have one Role, one Audience, and one Topic but several Formats.

RAFT Example

Role	Audience
A dog	The kid who owns him

Format	Topic
email	Complain about not going on long walks

Writing

To: Anna Banana
From: Sparky
RE: Long Walks

Hi Anna Banana,

We have been best friends for a long time. Remember when you were small and we would do everything together like play catch and take naps? My favorite thing was when we took long walks around the block. Now you act like you do not have time for me anymore. I want to take more long walks with you. Now! I really want to feel the fresh air, sniff all of the neighbors' trees, and spend time with you. Maybe you think you do not have time but I see you playing on your tablet and watching TV. If you do not take me on more long walks, I might start being best friends with your dad. Please do not make me do that!! Take me on a walk tomorrow please. I love you.

Your BFF,

Sparky

Name: _____ Date: _____

RAFT

Directions: Use this planner for your RAFT assignment.

Role	Audience

Format	Topic

Writing

Paragraph Frames

Objective

- Produce clear and coherent writing in which the development and organization are appropriate to task, purpose, and audience.

Background Information

Paragraph Frames (Nichols 1980) are effective scaffolds for emergent and developing writers across writing genres and content areas. Brozo and Simpson (2003) describe these frames as "skeletal paragraphs with strategically placed transitions or cue words that signal to students a particular way to think about and write about a concept" (272). This highly structured strategy consists of an outline of a paragraph that includes main ideas and key words that students can build on to write single paragraphs or put together to write longer stories, reports, essays, or other writing. Paragraph Frames help students learn the structure and organization of paragraphs, both in general and specific to a writing genre. Students develop skills in the use of transitional language, elaboration, rereading, and proofreading. For reluctant writers, framed writing eliminates the daunting experience of being faced with a blank page. As students advance in their skills, Paragraph Frames can be used to further develop word choice and elaboration skills.

Materials

- paragraph frame (created by teacher)

Process

1. Prepare for the lesson by creating or selecting a paragraph frame appropriate for the writing task.

2. Introduce the paragraph frame and discuss the elements of a paragraph. For example, a good paragraph has a topic sentence and three to five sentences that develop the topic. Discuss any transitional language or other important signal words and the use of a concluding statement.

3. Brainstorm ideas that can be used to complete the frame. This can be done with the whole class, or students can work with partners and then share ideas with the class.

4. Provide time for students to independently complete the frame to write a paragraph. Encourage students to elaborate, include long and short sentences, and use target vocabulary if appropriate.

5. Ask students to copy their paragraphs, paying attention to indentation and other structural elements, including punctuation. As students copy their work, they should reread, revise as desired, and check their spelling.

Differentiation

For students learning English, explicitly teach any academic language needed to complete the frame, such as the signal words or transitional language. Reading completed paragraphs aloud to a partner can strengthen speaking skills and use of academic language. Students who struggle with writing can revise and edit directly on the original piece rather than copying it.

Examples

My Favorite Dinner

If I could have my favorite dinner, these are the foods I would pick. First, I would pick _____ because _____. Next, I would select _____. I also like _____ because _____. I would be thrilled to have this dinner.

My Favorite Place

_____ is my favorite place. One reason is that _____. Another reason is that _____. _____ is also my favorite place because _____. There is no place as wonderful as _____.

Rehearsal

Objective

- With guidance and support from peers and adults, develop and strengthen writing as needed by planning, revising, and editing.

Background Information

Rehearsal (Graves 2003) refers to the first stage in the writing process, when writers engage in activities to activate their prior knowledge, generate and organize ideas, and collect words they will use to express these ideas. Rehearsal activities can take the form of conversations with peers, drawing, brainstorming, reading, or making lists. These are combined with traditional prewriting activities to spark students' creativity and help them organize their thoughts and plan for writing. This can be highly effective for students who struggle to get their creative juices flowing when using a graphic organizer for prewriting. The focus on narrowing and organizing helps students develop into more strategic writers (Tompkins 2018). Depending on the focus of the writing task and student differences, this lesson may need to be completed over successive days.

Materials

- graphic organizer to match the assignment (pages 148–152)

Process

1. Prepare by selecting a focus for the writing unit. If using the genre approach, select the genre and gather the instructional support materials needed. Open the unit with the Genre Analysis strategy (page 134). Select a graphic organizer that supports the genre (pages 148–152). If students will self-select a topic/genre, provide a generic cluster map to use for planning.

2. Select a rehearsal activity (page 147) for students that lends itself well to the writing task:

   - Brainstorming List
   - Brainstorming Cluster
   - Quickwrite
   - Quickdraw
   - Partner Discussion
   - Research and Take Notes

3. Explain the rehearsal activity and give students 10 to 15 minutes to complete it.

4. Direct students to review their rehearsal work and think about how they can organize their words and thoughts into ideas they can write about. Prompt students to think about how ideas and details go together or how they can sequence ideas or events they brainstormed. Provide students with the graphic organizer or generic cluster map to use for planning.

5. Have students complete the graphic organizers. Next, have students review their work and consider if the writing they planned is manageable in the amount of time and space they have and if it is too broad or too narrow. If the topic is too broad, students will have trouble keeping their writing focused, and if it is too narrow, they will not have enough to write about. Using the 5 W questions (Who? What? Where? When? Why?) can help students analyze their plans.

6. Students can then move to the drafting phase. Encourage them to revisit their Rehearsal work throughout the writing process to further develop their planning and organizational skills.

Differentiation

Students may initially need extensive modeling and scaffolding of this stage of the writing process. Providing students with mentor texts and engaging in backward mapping may help. Deconstructing mentor texts can illuminate the planning and organization behind the writing. Students may need support with transferring their Rehearsal ideas to the graphic organizers. Once students are familiar with this process, give them the opportunity to self-select the Rehearsal activity and the organizational structures that work best for them.

Examples of Rehearsal Activities

Brainstorming Lists Students brainstorm lists of words/phrases related to a topic. Encourage students to list as many words as they can even if they are not sure they are related. They can review once the list is complete or time is up to add or delete words/phrases.	**Brainstorming Clusters** Students create a cluster map of the words and ideas they have about the topic. Start with one word or idea at the center of the cluster, and write the related words around the central idea. As words spark student thinking of additional words and ideas, they draw a circle around the word that prompted the new cluster.	**Quickwrite** Students conduct a "free write" on the topic by writing continuously for five minutes, capturing anything they can think of about the topic. Once time is up, students can review the quickwrite to underline or highlight what they feel may be main ideas about the topic that they would like to pursue.
Quickdraw Students draw a picture or series of pictures about the topic to develop their main ideas and details for the writing. Encourage students to add as many details to the drawings as possible. These drawings can be revisited throughout the writing process.	**Partner Discussion** Students talk with partners about their ideas related to the topic. This can help students activate prior knowledge, elaborate on their ideas, and potentially clarify knowledge as they speak and listen to their partners. This can be used as a stand-alone Rehearsal or can accompany the brainstorming or quickwrite/draw activities.	**Research and Take Notes** Students can read more about the topic in print or online, view videos, or analyze images related to the topic. Note-taking should accompany the research, and students should be encouraged to generate questions to guide their research and planning.

Name: _____ Date: _____

Research Report

Directions: Use this planner to organize your research.

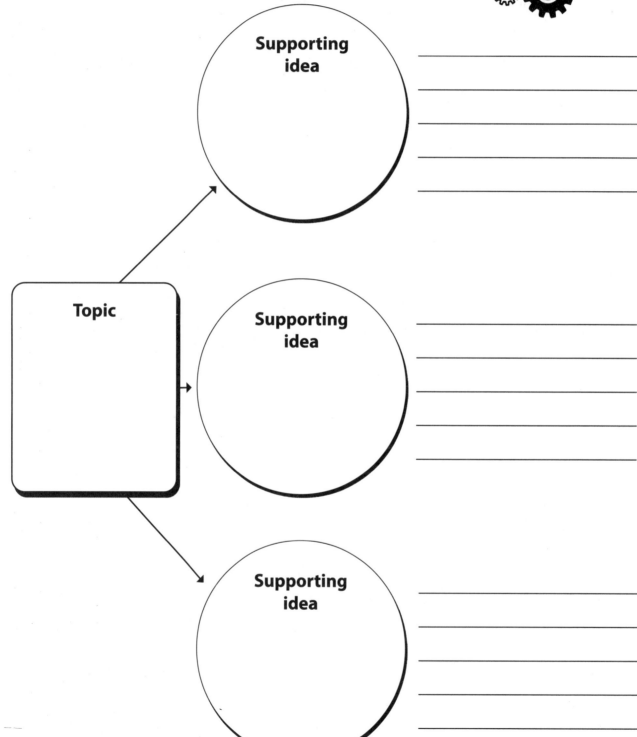

Name: _____ Date: _____

Summary Writing

Directions: Use this planner to organize your summary.

Main Idea

_____

_____

_____

Detail

_____

_____

Detail

_____

_____

Detail

_____

_____

Closing Statement

_____

_____

_____

Name: _____ Date: _____

Newspaper Article

Directions: Use this planner to organize your newspaper article.

Topic:_____

Who? ──

Who is the article about?_____

Who would be interested in reading it?_____

Who is the audience?_____

What? ───────────────────────────────────────

What is the purpose of the article?_____

_____

What is the main idea of the article?_____

_____

What is the author's desired result?_____

_____

When? ───────────────────────────────────────

When did the event in the news story take place?_____

Where? ──────────────────────────────────────

Where does the news story take place?_____

Where is the newspaper circulated?_____

Why? ──

Why did the events in the news story happen?_____

_____

_____

Name: _____ Date: _____

Persuasion Organizer

Directions: Use this planner to organize your persuasive argument. Write your position and the reasons. Provide details that support the reasons in the dotted boxes.

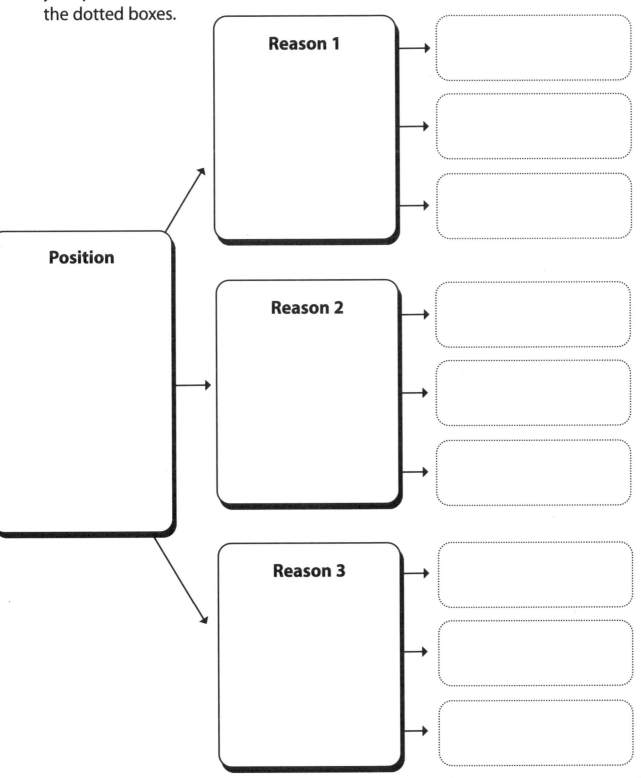

Name: _____ Date: _____

Story Mapping

Directions: Use this planner to organize your story.

Characters	Setting

Describe the problem(s)

Event 1	Event 2	Event 3

Describe the solution

Sentence Composing

Objectives

- Produce clear and coherent writing in which the development and organization are appropriate to task, purpose, and audience.

- Demonstrate command of the conventions of standard English grammar and usage when writing or speaking

Background Information

Sentence Composing (Killgallon and Killgallon 2000) offers four techniques to develop writers' skills in using a variety of sentence types, combining sentences, and overall composing. Using these techniques, students can learn to write like their favorite authors by using mentor sentences from favorite books as models. The techniques are *sentence unscrambling*, *sentence imitating*, *sentence combining*, and *sentence expanding*. Sentence Composing is effective because it makes writing improvement accessible by providing practice at the sentence level, combining grammar, syntax, and structure instruction with the power of mentor texts. Each technique is taught as a separate lesson. Model sentences can come from fiction and nonfiction texts.

Materials

- sentences from mentor text

Process

1. Prepare by selecting the technique for the lesson (see below). Choose several well-crafted sentences from a mentor text to use with the technique.

   - *Sentence unscrambling*: Break a sentence apart into smaller phrases. Students will put it back together to create a meaningful sentence and compare their result with the original.

   - *Sentence imitating*: Students write their own sentences that mimic the structure of the model sentence.

   - *Sentence combining*: Break a sentence into several short complete sentences (not phrases). Students will combine the short sentences into one meaningful complex sentence, then compare it to the mentor.

   - *Sentence expanding*: Choose a well-crafted sentence and share a meaningful part of it with students. Students expand on this part, creating a longer sentence and then comparing it to the original.

2. Introduce and explain the technique students will practice in this lesson.

3. Model the technique using a think-aloud to explain grammatical features you want students to notice (e.g., prepositional phrases, appositives, coordinating conjunctions). Elicit input from students as you model the technique.

4. Provide students with different sentences to practice the technique. After students use the technique, be sure to return to the original mentor sentence and compare it to students' results.

Differentiation

Students may benefit from the use of more tactile activities for the unscrambling and combining techniques. Provide students the parts of sentences on sentence strips to be unscrambled. The short sentences in the sentence combining activity and/or the sentence stem used for sentence expanding can be written on strips of paper students can manipulate. Have students work in pairs or small collaborative groups so they are supported by peers and can learn from one another. As students become more comfortable using each technique, create a "collection" of favorite sentences students find while reading to be used in future sentence composing lessons.

Examples

The following examples are from *Island of the Blue Dolphins* (O'Dell 1960).

Sentence Unscrambling

Mentor Sentence: "Everyone in our tribe had two names, the real one which was secret and was seldom used, and one which was common, for if people use your secret name it becomes worn out and loses its magic."

Sentence Parts

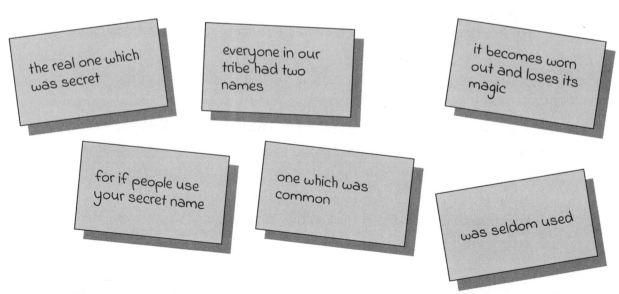

New Sentence: Everyone in our tribe had two names, one which was common and the real one which was secret was seldom used for if people use your secret name it becomes worn out and loses its magic.

Sentence Imitating

Mentor Sentence: "Since the beach was small and almost flooded when the tide was in, he asked if he could camp on higher ground."

New Sentence: Since my room was clean and vacuumed when my mom came home, I asked if I could play on my tablet.

Sentence Combining

Mentor Sentence: "The heavy seas and winds of winter drive the fish into deep water where they stay until the weather is settled and where they are hard to catch."

Short sentences

- The heavy seas drive the fish into deep water.
- The winds of winter drive the fish into deep water.
- The fish stay until the weather is settled.
- The fish stay where they are hard to catch.

New Sentence: The heavy seas and the winds of winter drive the fish into deep water and they are hard to catch because they stay there until the weather has settled.

Sentence Expanding

Mentor Sentence: "The women were cooking supper but all of them stopped and gathered around her, waiting for her to speak."

Stem: The women were cooking supper but all of them stopped . . .

New Sentence: The women were cooking supper but all of them stopped suddenly when they heard the sound of someone yelling for help in the distance.

Sentence Expansion

Objectives

- Produce clear and coherent writing in which the development and organization are appropriate to task, purpose, and audience.

- Use knowledge of language and its conventions when writing.

Background Information

Young writers tend to compose simplistic sentences that do not provide many details. In the primary grades, students focus on learning simple sentence construction: the pattern of the basic sentence (article, noun, verb) and the capitalization and punctuation necessary to begin and end a sentence. To continue to develop as writers, upper elementary students need explicit instruction in incorporating ideas and details into their writing. Sentence Expansion is a strategy to support students in making simple sentences more complex and interesting. Teaching students how to increase the complexity of their sentences has been shown to increase the quality of students' writing (Graham and Perin 2007).

Materials

- *Expanding Sentences* (page 158)
- sentences for modeling and practice

Process

1. Prepare for the lesson by selecting a simple sentence you will use for modeling and three to five sentences students will use for practice. In subsequent lessons, students can select simple sentences of their own during the revision stage of the writing process.

2. Explain to students that we can make our sentences more interesting by expanding them to include more ideas and details. Interesting sentences have details that allow the reader to picture what is occurring in the text. Remind students of what is needed to form a complete sentence.

3. Tell students that we can expand our sentences by providing more precise and detailed answers to questions such as: When? Where? How? Why?

4. Distribute *Expanding Sentences* to students. Using content from the classroom, present a simple sentence such as, "The student opened the door." Model the process by asking questions such as these:

   - When did the student open the door?

   - Where did the student open the door?

- Why did the student open the door?

- How did the student open the door?

5. Model answering and writing a response to each question. Think aloud to demonstrate the best place to insert the more precise language in the sentence. For example, if students respond "when the bell rang" to the question "When did the student open the door?" discuss ways to incorporate that detail: *When the bell rang, the student opened the door* or *The student opened the door when the bell rang.* Explain that if we add *When the bell rang* to the beginning of the sentence, it will be easier for us to provide even more details as we answer the other questions.

   Example

   Simple sentence: *The student opened the door.*

   Who/what (subject): The student

   Did what: opened the door

   How: quickly

   When: when the bell rang

   Where: in the classroom

   Why: it was time to go to recess

   Expanded sentence: *When the bell rang in the classroom, the student opened the door quickly because it was time to go to recess.*

6. Prompt students to read the expanded sentence aloud to be sure it makes grammatical sense.

7. Provide students additional sentences to practice the expanding technique. Students can work independently or in pairs. You may wish to provide word banks to direct students' attention toward adding specific types of words (verbs, adjectives, adverbs) or more precise language.

8. Have students share their expanded sentences with a small group or with the whole class. Be sure to return to the original sentences and compare them to students' expanded sentences.

Differentiation

Some students may benefit from a more tactile experience for expanding sentences. Provide sentence strips, cards with preprinted words and phrases, or laminated cards/sentence strips students can write on and manipulate to expand their sentences. Word banks may also be useful to prompt students to use specific words that have been taught previously.

Expanding Sentences

Directions: Expand sentences by adding details that answer the questions.

Simple sentence: _____

Who/what (subject): _____

Did what: _____

How: _____

When: _____

Where: _____

Why: _____

My expanded sentence: _____

_____

_____

● ●

Simple sentence: _____

Who/what (subject): _____

Did what: _____

How: _____

When: _____

Where: _____

Why: _____

My expanded sentence: _____

_____

_____

Revising Groups

Objective

- With guidance and support from peers and adults, develop and strengthen writing as needed by planning, revising, and editing.

Background Information

Revision may be the most rigorous and challenging part of the writing process. Often students—and sometimes teachers—combine revision and editing, but they are distinct processes. Revision is where the ideas from pre-writing and composing come to life and are clarified and distilled. During revision, students apply and refine their knowledge of structure, syntax, and word choice. Revising Groups (Mohr 1984; Tompkins 2018) allow students to work collaboratively on the task of revision, learning from and alongside peers, who may serve as models for writing and may even speed up the revision process. Modeling and scaffolding are necessary to teach students to work independently in groups. The steps below describe the independent, student-led process.

Materials

- *Revising Groups* (page 162)
- sentences for modeling and practice

Process

1. Provide each student with a *Revising Groups* activity sheet. Have students meet in collaborative groups of three to four students to share writing drafts. Each writer who will share should identify a few "trouble spots" or parts of their writing they want feedback on. They record these on the upper half of the activity sheet. Students will record feedback for their peers on the lower half of the activity sheet as they listen.

2. The first writer reads their draft aloud to the group while listeners make notes on their activity sheets of compliments and suggestions to share with the writer. Listeners may need to take a brief pause after the draft is read to collect their thoughts before sharing.

3. Listeners first offer compliments that focus on specific strengths of the writing or the topic and give examples. Teachers may need to model this several times to help students move from general comments such as, "I liked your story," to more specific comments such as, "The word *enormous* was a great choice when you described the bridge because it made me picture in my head how big it must have been."

4. The writer asks the group questions related to the trouble spots they had identified and the compliments they received. Listeners respond and offer their revision suggestions. Teachers may need to model ways to offer constructive feedback several times before students can do this independently.

5. Students repeat the process, taking turns reading their work and listening to others until each group member has shared.

6. Students cut the bottom half of the activity sheet into strips and give them to the appropriate group members. Each writer shares their plan for revision with the group, noting how they will revise their writing based on considering the feedback from the group members.

Differentiation

Some students may find it helpful to use sentence frames to provide feedback. Students who struggle with revision or who are reluctant writers will benefit from meeting with the teacher in a small group before meeting in revision groups. With teacher support, they can review their drafts and identify trouble spots to share with their revision groups. Additionally, teachers may want to participate in the revision groups, modeling and providing feedback until students are ready to work independently. Students who are ready for independence can be group leaders. As other students move toward mastery of the process, the group leaders can be rotated.

Revising Groups *Example*

My Trouble Spots

Did I use good words to describe how I felt when I lost my dog?

Does the part about my neighbor make sense?

Can you really picture what my dog looks like?

- -

My Active Listening

Directions: When your classmates are reading their work, listen and write compliments and suggestions for them.

Classmate's name: Julissa	My compliments: I liked when you said you were terrified while you waited in line because that's how I felt when I went on that big rollercoaster the first time.
	My suggestions: Tell the reader more about how it feels to be at an amusement park, like what does it smell like and what do you hear.
Classmate's name: Michael	My compliments: You did a good job telling us what the beach was like because if I close my eyes I can make a picture in my mind.
	My suggestions: I don't really understand how the lifeguard made the rescue, did they just swim in and save the guy or did they use a boat or a raft? Was the lifeguard a boy or a girl and did they do it by themselves?

Name: _____ Date: _____

Revising Groups

My Trouble Spots

Directions: Review your draft. Make notes of "trouble spots" or areas you would like feedback on.

_____

_____

_____

_____

_____

My Active Listening

Directions: When your classmates are reading their work, listen and write compliments and suggestions for them.

Classmate's name:	My compliments:
	My suggestions:
Classmate's name:	My compliments:
	My suggestions:

Picture This

Objectives

- Produce clear and coherent writing in which the development and organization are appropriate to task, purpose, and audience.

- Use knowledge of language and the conventions of standard English grammar when writing.

Background Information

Picture This is a strategy to develop students' use of descriptive language. Good writers choose precise words to convey their intended meaning. The right words help bring writing to life, enhance imagery, and clarify content. The importance of word choice is a powerful part of writing instruction. In Picture This, we focus on the way word choices enhance the mental images the reader sees. This lesson can be revisited and adapted to address specific types of words, focusing on adjectives, verbs, nouns, and so on to enhance students' writing.

Materials

- *Picture This* (page 166)
- sample sentences

Process

1. Select a focus for the lesson, and display four short example sentences. For instance, for a lesson on verbs, the teacher might display the following:

   - Josie walked to school.

   - Josie skipped to school.

   - Josie dashed to school.

   - Josie trudged to school.

2. Explain that each sentence describes Josie going to school, but the pictures created in our minds by each verb are quite different. The verb changes the message the author wants to convey.

3. Read the sentences again, stopping after each one, and allow students to act out how Josie is walking to underscore the difference word choice makes.

4. Explain to students that precise word choices enhance the visualization of a story, hook readers, and make writing more interesting to read.

5. Display a different sentence that uses a "boring" verb. Write the sentence again, leaving a blank space where the verb should be. Have students work with partners to add powerful, descriptive verbs to the sentence. Students may use a print or online thesaurus for help if necessary.

6. Ask the students to share their examples with the class. Make a list of some of their examples, highlighting the ways different verbs change the picture in our minds.

7. Give each student a *Picture This* activity sheet. Have students meet with partners and share a piece of their writing. Each student reviews their partner's writing to find examples of boring or plain verbs, recording them on the activity sheet. Partners then trade sheets and revise their own writing, using more precise verbs. Alternately, students could review their own writing for verbs that need revision.

Differentiation

Some students may need significant support generating lists of words (synonyms and word gradients) they can use to enhance sentences. Teachers may wish to pre-teach the lesson with select groups of students to help them create word banks to draw from later when working with partners. Additionally, some students may benefit from working in a teacher-led small group during the step when partners review one another's written pieces.

Picture This *Example*

Word Choice Focus: _adjective_

Sentences to Revise	New Sentences
It was a very (hot) day to go to a baseball game.	It was a scorching day to go to a baseball game.
The crowd seemed (tired) because of the heat and hardly anyone was cheering.	The crowd was listless and hardly anyone was cheering.
Matthew cooled off with a (cold) soda.	Matthew cooled off with an icy cold soda.

Name: _____ Date: _____

Picture This

Directions: Read your partner's writing. Copy sentences that need more precise words on the left side of this page. Circle the words that need to be replaced. Trade papers with your partner. On the right side of the page, revise the sentences using words that paint a sharper picture.

Word Choice Focus: _____

Sentences to Revise	New Sentences

REFERENCES

Almasi, Janice F., and Susan J. Hart. 2018. "Best Practices in Narrative Text Comprehension Instruction." In *Best Practice in Literacy Instruction*, 6th edition, edited by Lesley Mandel Morrow and Linda B. Gambrell, 221–249. New York: Guilford.

Anderson, Richard Chase, and P. David Pearson. 1984. "A Schema-Theoretic View of Basic Processes in Reading Comprehension." In *Handbook of Reading Research*, edited by P. David Pearson, with Rebecca Barr, Michael L. Kamil, and Peter Mosenthal, 255–291. New York: Routledge.

Anderson, Richard C., and William E. Nagy. 1992. "The Vocabulary Conundrum." *American Educator* 16 (4): 14–18, 44–47.

Armbruster, Bonnie B., Fran Lehr, and Jean Osborn. 2010. *Put Reading First: The Research Building Blocks for Teaching Children to Read: Kindergarten Through Grade 3*. 3rd edition. National Institute for Literacy.

August, Diane, Paola Uccelli, Lauren Artzi, Christopher Barr, David J. Francis. 2020. "English Learners' Acquisition of Academic Vocabulary: Instruction Matters, but So Do Word Characteristics." *Reading Research Quarterly* 56 (3): 559–582. doi.org/10.1002/rrq.323.

Baker, Linda, and Ann L. Brown. 1984. "Metacognitive Skills and Reading." In *Handbook of Reading Research*, edited by P. David. Pearson, Michael L. Kamil, Peter B. Mosenthal, and Rebecca Barr, 353–394. New York: Longman.

Barnes, Douglas, and Frankie Todd. 1995. *Communication and Learning Revisited*. Portsmouth, NH: Heinemann.

Baumann, James F., and Michael F. Graves. 2010. "What Is Academic Vocabulary?" *Journal of Adolescent & Adult Literacy* 54 (1): 4–12. doi.org/10.1598/jaal.54.1.1.

Bear, Donald R., and Diane M. Barone. 1998. *Developing Literacy: An Integrated Approach to Assessment and Instruction*. Boston, MA: Houghton Mifflin.

Bear, Donald R., Marcia Invernizzi, Shane Templeton, and Francine Johnston. 2020. *Words Their Way: Word Study for Phonics, Vocabulary, and Spelling Instruction*. 6th edition. Upper Saddle River, NJ: Pearson.

Beck, Isabel, Margaret G. McKeown, and Linda Kucan. 2002. *Bringing Words to Life: Robust Vocabulary Instruction*. New York: Guilford.

Bhattacharya, Alpana, and Linnea C. Ehri. 2004. "Graphosyllabic Analysis Helps Adolescent Struggling Readers Read and Spell Words." *Journal of Learning Disabilities* 37 (4): 331–348. doi.org/10.1177/00222194040370040501.

Blachowicz, Camille, and Peter Fisher. 2006. *Teaching Vocabulary in All Classrooms*. 3rd edition. Hoboken, NJ: Prentice Hall.

Bowers, Peter N., John R. Kirby, and S. Hélène Deacon. 2010. "The Effects of Morphological Instruction on Literacy Skills: A Systematic Review of the Literature." *Review of Educational Research* 80 (2): 144–179. doi.org/10.3102/0034654309359353.

Brozo, William G., and Michele L. Simpson. 2003. *Readers, Teachers, Learners: Expanding Literacy Across the Content Areas.* 4th edition. Upper Saddle River, NJ: Merrill.

Buehl, Doug. 2014. *Classroom Strategies for Interactive Learning.* 4th edition. Newark, DE: International Reading Association.

Cabell, Sonia Q., and HyeJin Hwang. 2020. "Building Content Knowledge to Boost Comprehension in the Primary Grades." *Reading Research Quarterly* 55 (S1): S99–S107. doi.org/10.1002/rrq.338.

Cappello, Marva, and Nancy T. Walker. 2021. "Talking Drawings: A Multimodal Pathway for Demonstrating Learning." *The Reading Teacher* 74 (4): 407–418. doi.org/10.1002/trtr.1952.

Cervetti, Gina N., Tanya S. Wright, and HyeJin Hwang. 2016. "Conceptual Coherence, Comprehension, and Vocabulary Acquisition: A Knowledge Effect?" *Reading and Writing* 29 (4): 761–779. doi.org/10.1007/s11145-016-9628-x.

Cromley, Jennifer G., and Roger Azevedo. 2007. "Testing and Refining the Direct and Inferential Mediation Model of Reading Comprehension." *Journal of Educational Psychology* 99 (2): 311–325. doi.org/10.1037/0022-0663.99.2.311.

Crosson, Amy C., Margaret G. McKeown, Puiwa Lei, Hui Zhao, Xinyue Li, Kelly Patrick, Kathleen Brown, and Yaqi Shen. 2021. "Morphological Analysis Skill and Academic Vocabulary Knowledge Are Malleable through Intervention and May Contribute to Reading Comprehension for Multilingual Adolescents." *Journal of Research in Reading* 44 (1): 154–174. doi.org/10.1111/1467-9817.12323.

Derewianka, Beverly. 2020. *Exploring How Texts Work.* 2nd edition. Newton, NSW: Primary English Teaching Association Australia.

Dewitz, Peter, Michael Graves, Bonnie Graves, and Connie Juel. 2020. *Teaching Reading in the 21st Century: Motivating All Learners.* 6th edition. Saddle River, NJ: Pearson.

Duke, Nell K., and Kelly B. Cartwright. 2021. "The Science of Reading Progresses: Communicating Advances Beyond the Simple View of Reading." *Reading Research Quarterly* (Special Issue) 56 (S1): 5–S44. doi.org/10.1002/rrq.411.

Duke, Nell K., and P. David Pearson. 2002. "Effective Practices for Developing Reading Comprehension." In *What Research Has to Say About Reading Instruction*, edited by Alan E. Farstrup and S. Jay Samuels, 3rd edition, 205–242. Newark, Delaware: International Reading Association.

Duke, Nell K., Alessandra E. Ward, and P. David Pearson. 2021. "The Science of Reading Comprehension Instruction." *The Reading Teacher* 74 (6): 663–672. doi.org/10.1002/trtr.1993.

Dunlap, Carmen Zuñiga, and Evelyn Marino Weisman. 2006. *Helping English Language Learners Succeed.* Huntington Beach, CA: Shell Education.

Durkin, Dolores. 1978. "What Classroom Observations Reveal About Reading Comprehension." *Reading Research Quarterly* 14 (4): 481–553. Newark, DE: International Reading Association.

Dutro, Susana, and Carrol Moran. 2003. "Rethinking English Language Instruction: An Architectural Approach." *English Learners: Reaching the Highest Level of English Literacy,* 227–258. doi.org/10.1598/0872074552.10.

Ehri, Linnea C. 2014. "Orthographic Mapping in the Acquisition of Sight Word Reading, Spelling Memory, and Vocabulary Learning." *Scientific Studies of Reading* 18 (1): 5–21. doi.org/10.1080/10888438.2013.819356.

Ehri, Linnea C., Simone R. Nunes, Steven A. Stahl, and Dale M. Willows. 2001. "Systematic Phonics Instruction Helps Students Learn to Read: Evidence from the National Reading Panel's Meta-Analysis." *Review of Educational Research* 71 (3): 393 –447. doi.org/10.3102/00346543071003393.

Fisher, Douglas, and Nancy Frey. 2008. *Word Wise and Content Rich, Grades 7-12: Five Essential Steps to Teaching Academic Vocabulary.* Portsmouth, NH: Heinemann.

———. 2014. "Closely Reading Informational Texts in the Primary Grades." *The Reading Teacher* 68 (3): 222–227. doi.org/10.1002/trtr.1317.

———. 2020. *Improving Adolescent Literacy: Content Area Strategies at Work.* 5th edition. Upper Saddle River, NJ: Pearson Education.

Fitzgerald, Jill, and Timothy Shanahan. 2000. "Reading and Writing Relations and Their Development." *Educational Psychologist* 35 (1): 39–50. doi.org/10.1207/s15326985ep3501_5.

Gahn, Shelley Mattson. 1989. "A Practical Guide for Teaching Writing in the Content Areas." *Journal of Reading* 32 (6): 525–531.

Gough, Philip B., and William E. Tunmer. 1986. "Decoding, Reading, and Reading Disability." *Remedial and Special Education* 7 (1): 6–10.

Gourgey, Annette F. 1998. "Metacognition in Basic Skills Instruction." *Instructional Science* 26 (1/2): 81–96. Philadelphia: Kluwer Academic Publishers. doi.org/10.1023/a:1003092414893.

Graham, Steve. 2020. "The Sciences of Reading and Writing Must Become More Fully Integrated." *Reading Research Quarterly* 55 (S1): S35–S44. doi.org/10.1002/rrq.332.

Graham, Steve, Alisha Bollinger, Carol Booth Olson, Catherine D'Aoust, Charles MacArthur, Deborah McCutchen, Natalie and Olinghouse. 2012a. *Teaching Elementary School Students to Be Effective Writers: A Practice Guide* (NCEE 20124058). Washington, DC: National Center for Education Evaluation and Regional Assistance, Institute of Education Sciences, U.S. Department of Education. Retrieved from ies.ed.gov/ncee/wwc/publications_reviews.aspx#pubsearch.

Graham, Steve, and Michael Hebert. 2010. *Writing to Read: Evidence for How Writing Can Improve.* A Carnegie Corporation Time to Act Report. Washington, DC: Alliance for Excellent Education.

Graham, Steve, Debra McKeown, Sharlene Kiuhara, and Karen R. Harris. 2012b. "A Meta-Analysis of Writing Instruction for Students in the Elementary Grades." *Journal of Educational Psychology* 104 (4): 879–896. doi.org/10.1037/a0029185.

Graham, Steve, and Dolores Perin. 2007. "A Meta-Analysis of Writing Instruction for Adolescent Students." *Journal of Educational Psychology*, 99 (3): 445–476. doi.org/10.1037/0022-0663.99.3.445.

Graves, Donald H. 2003. *Writing: Teachers & Children at Work.* 20th Anniversary Edition. Portsmouth, NH: Heinemann.

Gutiérrez, Gabriel, and Mike L. Vanderwood. 2013. "A Growth Curve Analysis of Literacy Performance Among Second-Grade, Spanish-Speaking, English-Language Learners." *School Psychology Review*, edited by Benjamin Silberglitt, 42 (1): 3–21. doi.org/10.1080/02 796015.2013.12087488.

Hacker, Douglas J., Dunlosky, John, and Arthur C. Graesser. 1998. *Metacognition in Educational Theory and Practice.* Mahwah, NJ: L. Erlbaum Associates.

Halliday, M. A. K. 1975. *Learning How to Mean: Explorations in the Development of Language.* London: Edward Arnold.

Harvey, Stephanie, and Anne Goudvis. 2017. *Strategies That Work: Teaching Comprehension for Engagement, Understanding, and Building Knowledge, Grades K–8.* 3rd edition. Portland, ME: Stenhouse.

Hattie, John. 2009. *Visible Learning: A Synthesis of Over 800 Meta-Analyses Relating to Achievement.* New York: Routledge.

Hirsch, E. D. 2006. "Building Knowledge: The Case for Bringing Content into the Language Arts Block and for a Knowledge-Rich Curriculum Core for All Children." *American Educator*, Spring 2006. American Federation of Teachers. aft.org/periodical /american-educator/spring-2006/building-knowledge.

Hochman, Judith C., and Natalie Wexler. 2017. "One Sentence at a Time: The Need for Explicit Instruction in Teaching Students to Write Well." *American Educator,* Summer 2017. American Federation of Teachers. aft.org/ae/summer2017/hochman-wexler.

Hollie, Sharroky. 2018. *Culturally and Linguistically Responsive Teaching and Learning, Second Edition.* Huntington Beach, CA: Shell Education.

Hoover, Wesley A., and Philip B. Gough. 1990. "The Simple View of Reading." *Reading and Writing: An Interdisciplinary Journal* 2 (2): 127–160. doi.org/10.1007/BF00401799.

Hoover, Wesley A., and William E. Tunmer. 2018. "The Simple View of Reading: Three Assessments of Its Adequacy." *Remedial and Special Education* 39 (5): 304–312. *Crossref,* doi.org/10.1177/0741932518773154.

———. 2020. *The Cognitive Foundations of Reading and Its Acquisition: A Framework with Applications Connecting Teaching and Learning (Literacy Studies).* London: Springer.

Hoover, Wesley A., and William E. Tunmer. 2022. "The Primacy of Science in Communicating Advances in the Science of Reading." *Reading Research Quarterly* (57) 2: 399–408. doi.org/10.1002/rrq.446.

Horton, Phillip B., Andrew A. McConney, Michael Gallo, Amanda L. Woods, Gary J. Senn, and Denis Hamelin. 1993. "An Investigation of the Effectiveness of Concept Mapping as an Instructional Tool." *Science Education* 77 (1): 95–111. doi.org/10.1002/sce.3730770107.

Hoyt, Linda. 2002. *Make It Real: Strategies for Success with Informational Texts.* Portsmouth, NH: Heinemann.

Hulit, Lloyd M., Merle R. Howard, and Kathleen R. Fahey. 2018. *Born to Talk: An Introduction to Speech and Language Development.* 7th edition. Boston, MA: Allyn and Bacon.

Jackson, Julie K., Margarita Huerta, and Tiberio Garza. 2020. "A Promising Science and Literacy Instructional Model with Hispanic Fifth Grade Students." *The Journal of Educational Research* 113 (2): 79–92. doi.org/10.1080/00220671.2020.1728734.

Jouhar, Mohammed R., and William H. Rupley. 2020. "The Reading–Writing Connection based on Independent Reading and Writing: A Systematic Review." *Reading & Writing Quarterly* 37 (2): 136–156. doi.org/10.1080/10573569.2020.1740632.

Jump, Jennifer, and Robin D. Johnson. 2023. *What the Science of Reading Says about Word Recognition.* Huntington Beach, CA: Shell Education.

Jump, Jennifer, and Kathleen Kopp. 2023. *What the Science of Reading Says about Reading Comprehension and Content Knowledge.* Huntington Beach, CA: Shell Education.

Jump, Jennifer, and Hillary Wolfe. 2023. *What the Science of Reading Says about Writing.* Huntington Beach, CA: Shell Education.

Kamil, Michael L., Geoffrey D. Borman, Janice Dole, Cathleen C. Kral, Terry Salinger, and Joseph Torgesen. 2008. *Improving Adolescent Literacy: Effective Classroom and Intervention Practices: A Practice Guide* (NCEE #2008-4027). Washington, DC: National Center for Education Evaluation and Regional Assistance, Institute of Education Sciences, U.S. Department of Education.

Kearns, Devin M., Laura M. Steacy, Donald L. Compton, Jennifer K. Gilbert, Amanda P. Goodwin, Eunsoo Cho, Esther R. Lindstrom, and Alyson A. Collins. 2014. "Modeling Polymorphemic Word Recognition." *Journal of Learning Disabilities* 49 (4): 368–394. doi.org/10.1177/0022219414554229.

Killgallon, Donald, and Jenny Killgallon. 2000. *Sentence Composing for Elementary School: A Worktext to Build Better Sentences.* Portsmouth, NH: Heinemann.

Kilpatrick, David A. 2015. *Essentials of Assessing, Preventing, and Overcoming Reading Difficulties (Essentials of Psychological Assessment).* Hoboken, NJ: John Wiley & Sons.

Kintsch, Walter. 1988. "The Role of Knowledge in Discourse Comprehension: A Construction-Integration Model." *Psychological Review* 95 (2): 163–82. doi.org/10.1037/0033-295x.95.2.163.

———. 2018. "Revisiting the Construction—Integration Model of Text Comprehension and Its Implications for Instruction." In *Theoretical Models and Processes of Literacy,* edited by Donna E. Alvermann, Norman J. Unrau, Misty Sailors, and Robert B. Ruddell, 178–203. New York: Routledge.

Koster, Monica, Elena Tribushinina, Peter F. de Jong, Huub van den Bergh. 2015. "Teaching Children to Write: A Meta-Analysis of Writing Intervention Research." *Journal of Writing Research* 7 (2): 249–274. doi.org/10.17239/jowr-2015.07.02.2.

Krashen, Stephen. 2009. "81 Generalizations about Free Voluntary Reading." IATEFL Young Learner and Teenager Special Interest Group Publication. successfulenglish.com /wp-content/uploads/2010/01/81-Generalizations-about-FVR-2009.pdf.

LeVasseur, Valerie Marciarille, Paul Macaruso, and Donald Shankweiler. 2008. "Promoting Gains in Reading Fluency: A Comparison of Three Approaches." *Reading and Writing* 21 (3): 205–230. doi.org/10.1007/s11145-007-9070-1.

Levesque, Kyle C., Michael J. Kieffer, and S. Hélène Deacon. 2017. "Morphological Awareness and Reading Comprehension: Examining Mediating Factors." *Journal of Experimental Child Psychology* 160: 1–20. doi.org/10.1016/j.jecp.2017.02.015.

Moats, Louisa C. 2020. "Teaching Reading Is Rocket Science." *American Educator,* Summer 2020. aft.org/ae/summer2020/moats.

———. 2022. *LETRS Language Essentials for Teachers of Reading and Spelling: Module 2, The Speech Sounds of English: Phonetics, Phonology, and Phoneme Awareness.* Dallas, TX: Lexia Learning.

Mohr, Marian. 1984. *Revision: The Rhythm of Meaning.* Portsmouth, NH: Heinemann.

Morrow, Lesley Mandel. 2003. "Motivating Lifelong Voluntary Readers." In *Handbook of Research on Teaching the English Language Arts,* edited by James Flood, Diane Lapp, James R. Squire, and Julie M. Jenson, 857–67. Mahwah, NJ: Lawrence Erlbaum Associates.

Murphy, Kimberly A., and Laura M. Justice. 2019. "Lexical-Level Predictors of Reading Comprehension in Third Grade: Is Spelling a Unique Contributor?" *American Journal of Speech-Language Pathology* 28 (4): 1597–1610. doi.org/10.1044/2019_ajslp-18-0299.

Nagy, William, Virginia W. Berninger, and Robert D. Abbott. 2006. "Contributions of Morphology Beyond Phonology to Literacy Outcomes of Upper Elementary and Middle-School Students." *Journal of Educational Psychology* 98 (1): 134–147. doi.org/10.1037/0022-0663.98.1.134.

Nagy, William E., Joanne F. Carlisle, and Amanda P. Goodwin. 2013. "Morphological Knowledge and Literacy Acquisition." *Journal of Learning Disabilities* 47 (1): 3–12. doi.org/10.1177/0022219413509967.

National Early Literacy Panel. 2008. *Developing Early Literacy: Report of the National Early Literacy Panel: A Scientific Synthesis of Early Literacy Development and Implications for Intervention.* Jessup, MD: National Institute for Literacy with National Center for Family Literacy.

National Governors Association Center for Best Practices, Council of Chief State School Officers. 2010. *Common Core State Standards for English Language Arts.* Washington, DC: National Governors Association Center for Best Practices, Council of Chief State School Officers.

National Reading Panel (U.S.) and National Institute of Child Health and Human Development (U.S.). 2000. *Report of the National Reading Panel: Teaching Children to Read: An Evidence-based Assessment of the Scientific Research Literature on Reading and Its Implications for Reading Instructio*n. Bethesda: U.S. Dept. of Health and Human Services, Public Health Service, National Institutes of Health, National Institute of Child Health and Human Development.

Neuman, Susan B., Tanya Kaefer, and Ashley Pinkham. 2014. "Building Background Knowledge." *Reading Teacher* 68 (2): 145–148. jstor.org/stable/24573715.

Nichols, James N. 1980. "Using Paragraph Frames to Help Remedial High School Students with Written Assignments." *The Journal of Reading* 24 (3): 228–231.

Paige, David D., Timothy Rasinski, Theresa Magpuri-Lavell, Grant S. Smith. 2014. "Interpreting the Relationships Among Prosody, Automaticity, Accuracy, and Silent Reading Comprehension in Secondary Students." *Journal of Literacy Research* 46 (2): 123–56. doi.org/10.1177/1086296x14535170.

Palincsar, Annemarie Sullivan, and Deborah A. Brown. 1987. "Enhancing Instructional Time Through Attention to Metacognition." *Journal of Learning Disabilities* 20 (2): 66–75. Thousand Oaks, CA: SAGE Publications. doi.org/10.1177/002221948702000201.

Paris, Scott G., Marjorie Y. Lipson, and Karen K. Wixson. 1983. "Becoming a Strategic Reader." *Contemporary Educational Psychology* 8 (3): 293–316. doi.org/10.1016/0361-476x(83)90018-8.

Perfetti, Charles A. 1995. "Cognitive Research Can Inform Reading Education." *Journal of Research in Reading* 18 (2): 106-115.

———. 1998. "Two Basic Questions about Reading and Learning to Read." In *Problems and Interventions in Literacy Development*, edited by Pieter Reitsma and Ludo Verhoeven, 15–48. Dordrecht, The Netherlands: Kluwer Academic Publishers.

Perfetti, Charles A., Ying Liu, Julie Fiez, Jessica Nelson, Donald J. Bolger, and Li-Hai Tan. 2007. "Reading in Two Writing Systems: Accommodation and Assimilation of the Brain's Reading Network." *Bilingualism: Language and Cognition* 10 (2): 131–46. doi.org/10.1017/s1366728907002891.

Perfetti, Charles, and Joseph Stafura. 2013. "Word Knowledge in a Theory of Reading Comprehension." *Scientific Studies of Reading* 18 (1): 22–37. doi.org/10.1080/10888438.2 013.827687.

Pressley, Michael, and Peter Afflerbach. 1995. *Verbal Protocols of Reading: The Nature of Constructively Responsive Reading.* New York: Routledge.

Pressley, Michael, John G. Borkowski, and Wolfgang Schneider. 1987. "Cognitive Strategies: Good Strategy Users Coordinate Metacognition and Knowledge." *Annals of Child Development* 4: 89–129.

Pressley, Michael, Sara E. Dolezal, Lisa M. Raphael, Lindsey Mohan, Alysia D. Roehrig, and Kristen Bogner. 2003. *Motivating Primary-Grade Students.* New York: Guilford.

Rasinski, Timothy V., Nancy Padak, Joanna Newton, and Evangeline Newton. 2011. "The Latin-Greek Connection." *The Reading Teacher* 65 (2): 133–141. doi.org/10.1002 /trtr.01015.

Rasinski, Timothy, David Paige, Cameron Rains, Fran Stewart, Brenda Julovich, Deb Prenkert, William H. Rupley, and William Dee Nichols. 2017. "Effects of Intensive Fluency Instruction on the Reading Proficiency of Third-Grade Struggling Readers." *Reading & Writing Quarterly* 33 (6): 519–532. doi.org/10.1080/10573569.2016.1250144.

Rasinski, Timothy, Kasim Yildirim, James Nageldinger. 2011. "Building Fluency Through the Phrased Text Lesson." *The Reading Teacher* 65 (4): 252–255. doi.org/10.1002 /TRTR.01036.

Rupley, William H., Logan, and William D. Nichols. 1999. "Vocabulary Instruction in a Balanced Reading Program." *The Reading Teacher*, 52 (4), 336–346. Newark, DE: International Reading Association.

Ryder, Randall J., and Michael F. Graves. 2003. *Reading and Learning in Content Areas.* 3rd edition. Hoboken, NJ: John Wiley & Sons.

Santa, Carol M., Lynn T. Havens, and Bonnie J. Valdes. 1995. *Project CRISS (Creating Independence Through Student-Owned Strategies).* 3rd edition. Dubuque, IA: Kendall /Hunt.

Scarborough, Hollis S. 2001. "Connecting Early Language and Literacy to Later Reading (Dis)abilities: Evidence, Theory, and Practice." In *Handbook of Early Literacy Research,* edited by Susan B. Neuman and David K. Dickinson, 97–110. New York: The Guilford Press.

Schmidt, Claudia Janin Brandenburg, Jenny Busch, Gerhard Büttner, Dietmar Grube, Claudia Mähler, and Marcus Hasselhorn. 2021. "Developmental Trajectories of Phonological Information Processing in Upper Elementary Students with Reading or Spelling Disabilities." *Reading Research Quarterly* 56 (1): 143–171. doi.org/10.1002 /rrq.299.

Sedita, Joan. 2019. "The Strands That Are Woven into Skilled Writing." keystoliteracy.com/ wp-content/uploads/2020/02/The-Strands-That-Are-Woven-Into-Skilled-WritingV2.pdf.

Shanahan, Timothy. 2018. "Where Questioning Fits Comprehension: Skills and Strategies." Reading Rockets: Shanahan on Literacy (blog), June 1, 2018. readingrockets.org/blogs /English-literacy/where-questioning-fits-comprehension-instruction-skills-and-strategies.

Shanahan, Timothy, Kim Callison, Christine Carriere, Nell K. Duke, P. David Pearson, Christopher Schatschneider, and Joseph Torgesen. 2010. *Improving Reading Comprehension in Kindergarten through 3rd Grade: A Practice Guide* (NCEE 2010-4038). Washington, DC: National Center for Education Evaluation and Regional Assistance, Institute of Education Sciences, U.S. Department of Education.

Shefelbine, J., and J. Calhoun. 1991. "Variability in Approaches to Identifying Polysyllabic Words: A Descriptive Study of Sixth Graders with Highly, Moderately, and Poorly Developed Syllabification Strategies." *Learner Factors/Teacher Factors: Issues in Literacy Research and Instruction*, edited by J. Zutell and S. McCormick, 169–177. Chicago, IL: National Reading Conference.

Shefelbine, John, and Katherine K. Newman. 2004. *SIPPS: Systematic Instruction in Phoneme Awareness, Phonics, and Sight Words KIT: (Two Books: Challenge Level Polysyllabic Decoding and Decoding Manual Program Overview; Two Wall Charts, and 127 Sight Syllable Cards) (Challenge Level Polysyllabic Decoding).* 2nd edition. Oakland, CA: Developmental Studies Center.

Sinatra, Richard, Vicky Zygouris-Coe, and Sheryl B. Dasinger. 2012. "Preventing a Vocabulary Lag: What Lessons Are Learned from Research." *Reading and Writing Quarterly* 28 (4): 333–357. doi.org/10.1080/10573569.2012.702040

Singer, Bonnie D., and Anthony S. Bashir. 2004. "EmPOWER: A Strategy for Teaching Students with Language Learning Disabilities How to Write Expository Text." In *Language and Literacy Learning in Schools*, edited by Elaine R. Silliman and Louise Wilkinson, 239–72. New York: The Guilford Press.

Snow, Catherine E. 2018. "Simple and Not-So-Simple Views of Reading." *Remedial and Special Education* 39 (5): 313–316. doi.org/10.1177/0741932518770288.

Snow, Catherine E., and Connie Juel. 2005. "Teaching Children to Read: What Do We Know about How to Do It?" In *The Science of Reading: A Handbook*, edited by Margaret J. Snowling and Charles Hulme, 501–520. Oxford: Blackwell. doi.org/10.1002/9780470757642.ch26.

Sticht, Thomas G., and James H. James. 1984. "Listening and Reading." In *Handbook of Reading Research*, edited by P. David Pearson, with Rebecca Barr, Michael L. Kamil, and Peter Mosenthal, 293–318. New York: Routledge.

Tomlinson, Carol A. 2014. *The Differentiated Classroom: Responding to the Needs of All Learners*. 2nd edition. Alexandria, VA: ASCD.

Tompkins, Gail. 2018. *Teaching Writing: Balancing Process and Product*. 7th edition. Saddle River, NJ: Pearson.

Toste, Jessica R., Kelly J. Williams, and Philip Capin. 2016. "Reading Big Words: Instructional Practices to Promote Multisyllabic Word Reading Fluency." *Intervention in School and Clinic* 52 (5): 270–278. doi.org/10.1177/1053451216676797.

Wanzek, Jeanne, Elizabeth A. Stevens, Kelly J. Williams, Nancy Scammacca, Sharon Vaugh, and Katherine Sargent. 2018. "Current Evidence on the Effects of Intensive Early Reading Interventions." *Journal of Learning Disabilities* 51 (6): 612–624. doi.org/10.1177/0022219418775110.

Wattenberg, Ruth. 2016. "Inside the Common Core Reading Tests: Why the Best Prep Is a Knowledge-Rich Curriculum." *Knowledge Matters*, Issue Brief #7, September 2016, knowledgematterscampaign.org/wp-content/uploads/2016/09/Wattenberg.pdf.

Wexler, Natalie. 2019. *The Knowledge Gap: The Hidden Cause of America's Broken Education System—and How to Fix It*. New York: Penguin/Random House.

Willingham, Daniel T. 2006. "How Knowledge Helps: It Speeds and Strengthens Reading Comprehension, Learning—and Thinking." *American Educator*, Spring 2006. American Federation of Teachers. aft.org/periodical/american-educator/spring-2006/how-knowledge-helps.

Zwiers, Jeff. 2022. *Building Academic Language: Essential Practices for Content Classrooms, Grades 5–12*. San Francisco: Jossey-Bass.

Affixes

Prefixes	Meanings	Examples
anti–	against	antiwar
de–	down, off of	destroy
dis–	not, apart	disagree
en(m)–	in, on	encode, embrace
fore–	outside	forecast
in(m)–	in	intake, implant
in–, im–, il–, ir–	not	injustice, impossible, illiterate, irregular
inter–	between	interact
mid–	middle	midway
mis–	wrongly	mistake
non–	not	nonsense
over–	excessive, above	overlook
pre–	before	preview
re–	again	return
semi–	half	semicircle
sub–	under	submarine
super–	above	superstar
trans–	across	transport
un–	not	unfriendly
under–	under	undercover

Affixes *(cont.)*

Suffixes	Meanings	Examples
–able, –ible	can be done	doable
–al, –ial	quality, relation	personal
–ar, –er, –or	one who	beggar, doer, actor
–ed	past verb	turned
–en	material, make	golden
–er	more	higher
–est	most	best, biggest
–ful	full of	careful, joyful
–ic	quality, relation	linguistic
–ing	present participle	running
–(t)ion	condition, action	action
–(i)ty	state of	infinity, sanity
–(t)ive	having the quality of	motive, votive
–less	without	fearless, careless
–ly	having	quickly, quietly
–ment	mental, mention	enjoyment
–ness	state of	kindness
–ous	full of	joyous, religious
–s	more than one	books
–y	having	happy, windy

Spelling Generalizations for Adding Suffixes

Double the Consonant

- Double the consonant in words that contain a short vowel followed by a consonant. This retains the CVC pattern in the first syllable (don't double *w*, *x*, or *y*).
    - shop > shopping, shopped
    - run > running, runner

Silent *e*

- Drop the silent *e* at the end of a word when adding a vowel suffix.
    - drive > driving, driver
    - make > making, maker
- Keep the silent *e* at the end of a word when adding a consonant suffix.
    - grace > graceful
    - home > homeless

Rule for Ys

- Change the *y* to an *i* in words that end in a consonant and *y*, except when adding *–ing*.
    - happy > happiest, happier
    - marry > married, marrying
- Keep the *y* in words that end with *y* and have a vowel before the *y*.
    - play > playing, played
    - enjoy > enjoyed, enjoyment

Digital Resources

Accessing the Digital Resources

The digital resources can be downloaded by following these steps:

1. Go to www.tcmpub.com/digital

2. Use the 13-digit ISBN number to redeem the digital resources.

3. Respond to the question using the book.

4. Follow the prompts on the Content Cloud website to sign in or create a new account.

5. The content redeemed will appear on your My Content screen. Click on the product to look through the digital resources. All file resources are available for download. Select files can be previewed, opened, and shared. Any web-based content, such as videos, links, or interactive text, can be viewed and used in the browser but is not available for download.

For questions and assistance, please contact Teacher Created Materials.

email: customerservice@tcmpub.com

phone: 800-858-7339

Contents of the Digital Resources

The digital resources include templates for the student activity pages in this book.